FILMMAKERS SERIES
edited by
ANTHONY SLIDE

24. *The Films of Freddie Francis,* by Wheeler Winston Dixon. 1991
25. *Hollywood Be Thy Name,* by William Bakewell. 1991
26. *The Charm of Evil: The Life and Films of Terence Fisher,* by Wheeler Winston Dixon. 1991
27. *Lionheart in Hollywood: The Autobiography of Henry Wilcoxon,* with Katherine Orrison. 1991
28. *William Desmond Taylor: A Dossier,* by Bruce Long. 1991
29. *The Films of Leni Riefenstahl,* 2nd ed., by David B. Hinton. 1991
30. *Hollywood Holyland: The Filming and Scoring of "The Greatest Story Ever Told,"* by Ken Darby. 1992
31. *The Films of Reginald LeBorg; Interviews, Essays, and Filmography,* by Wheeler Winston Dixon. 1992
32. *Memoirs of a Professional Cad,* by George Sanders, with Tony Thomas. 1992
33. *The Holocaust in French Film,* by André Pierre Colombat. 1993
34. *Robert Goldstein and "The Spirit of '76,"* edited and compiled by Anthony Slide. 1993
35. *Those Were the Days, My Friend: My Life in Hollywood with David O. Selznick and Others,* by Paul Macnamara. 1993
36. *The Creative Producer,* by David Lewis; edited by James Curtis. 1993
37. *Reinventing Reality: The Art and Life of Rouben Mamoulian,* by Mark Spergel. 1993
38. *Malcolm St. Clair: His Films, 1915–1948,* by Ruth Anne Dwyer. 1997
39. *Beyond Hollywood's Grasp: American Filmmakers Abroad, 1914–1945,* by Harry Waldman. 1994
40. *A Steady Digression to a Fixed Point,* by Rose Hobart. 1994
41. *Radical Juxtaposition: The Films of Yvonne Rainer,* by Shelley Green. 1994
42. *Company of Heroes: My Life as an Actor in the John Ford Stock Company,* by Harry Carey, Jr. 1994
43. *Strangers in Hollywood: A History of Scandinavian Actors in American Films from 1910 to World War II,* by Hans J. Wollstein. 1994
44. *Charlie Chaplin: Intimate Close-Ups,* by Georgia Hale, edited with an introduction and notes by Heather Kiernan. 1995
45. *The Word Made Flesh: Catholicism and Conflict in the Films of Martin Scorsese,* by Michael Bliss. 1995
46. *W. S. Van Dyke's Journal: White Shadows in the South Seas (1927–1928) and other Van Dyke on Van Dyke,* edited and annotated by Rudy Behlmer. 1996

The author, 1989. (Photo courtesy of Bill Rapf, Amherst, NH)

Back Lot

Growing Up with the Movies

Maurice Rapf

Filmmakers Series
No. 64

The Scarecrow Press, Inc.
Lanham, Maryland, & London
1999

SCARECROW PRESS, INC.

Published in the United States of America
by Scarecrow Press, Inc.
4720 Boston Way
Lanham, Maryland 20706

4 Pleydell Gardens, Folkestone
Kent CT20 2DN, England

British Library Cataloguing in Publication Information Available

Library of Congress Cataloging-in-Publication Data

Rapf, Maurice, 1914–
    Back lot : growing up with the movies / Maurice Rapf.
       p.   cm. — (Filmmakers series ; no. 64)
    Includes index.
    ISBN 0-8108-3583-5 (cloth : alk. paper)
    1. Rapf, Maurice, 1914– .   2. Motion picture producers and
directors—United States—Biography.   3. Screenwriters—United
States—Biography.   I. Title.   II. Series.
PN1998.3.R373A3   1999
791.43′ 0233′ 092—dc21
                                               98-34656
                                                CIP

♾ ™ The paper used in this publication meets the minimum requirements
of American National Standard for Information Sciences—Permanence of
Paper for Printed Library Materials, ANSI Z39.48—1984.
Manufactured in the United States of America.

This book is dedicated to the memory of my beloved wife, Louise, and to all my former students whose passion for the movies caused me to remember.

And with gratitude to Anthony Slide for his scrupulous reading and correction of the manuscript.

MAURICE RAPF
—born 1914
— died 2003
(age 89)

Contents

List of Illustrations

Introduction

What I know about the movie industry and its films was learned from firsthand experience and not from books. I saw movie production evolve from its origins on the East Coast to its culmination in Hollywood, from silent pictures to sound, and from being a fun-loving frontier community to being a huge and fiercely competitive industry. Its paternal, family atmosphere changed to one marked by bitter struggles against Eastern bankers and against the formation of craft unions. An apolitical never-never land became a community very much aware of—and nervous about—its social responsibility in a period of economic depression, when world peace was seriously threatened by fascist aggression.

This, then, was my background, and it explains why the movies and the movie business have been the dominant influences on my life since my childhood in New York City. This book is a stab at autobiography with some of the stories drawn from lectures to college film classes during the past thirty years.

I often tell students in film studies that the fatal but inevitable flaw in recorded movie history is that we are dealing with a highly publicized industry and that the story of that industry, the information about its leading characters, is too often fabricated by press agentry and the hoopla of public relations. So how can we trust what history—based on artificially nurtured interviews and puff pieces—tells us about the personalities that have dominated the movies?

The power of publicity is well illustrated by the lack of information about some of the women pioneers like Alice Guy Blaché. This French woman was a secretary working for Gaumont in Paris when she made a film in 1896 which was probably the first story film directed by anyone of either sex. Ms. Blaché made hundreds of films after that and died in the United States, but because no press agents have promoted her work, most film historians have largely ignored her (see, however, Scarecrow Press's *The Memoirs of Alice Guy Blaché,* 2nd edition, 1996).

The same is true of Nell Shipman, who started her career as an actress rivaling Mary Pickford and Lillian Gish and moved to the directorial ranks as an independent but refused industry contracts in the 1910s to pursue her independent role as a maker of nature films in Idaho. And in my early days at MGM I was very aware of the many early women writers who are largely unknown today—Lenore Coffee, Zelda Sears, Florence Ryerson, Eve Greene, Marion Jackson, Sylvia Thalberg, and, of course, Frances Marion. Likewise, two of the most sought after film editors on the MGM lot were Blanche Sewell and Margaret Booth and the dominant figure in the story department during her much too short lifetime was the very knowledgeable Stanford graduate, Kate Corbaley.

I should also mention a man, Oscar Micheaux, who wrote, directed, produced, and edited forty feature films for black audiences between 1920 and 1950. He would be virtually unknown—because only one or two of his films still exist—except for the scholarly work of a few people. (See, for example, Donald Bogle's book, *Coons, Mulattoes, Mammies and Bucks: An Interpretive History of Blacks in American Films,* Continuum, 1994)

For the most part, however, if an individual receives no press plugs, he or she soon ceases to exist. How many times have you read in movie gossip columns, "What young movie queen whose initials are BH has been seen four nights in a row with what handsome young leading man whose initials are SP?" Or, Ethan Hawke quoted as saying, "A roomful of people looking at me is my idea of heaven." Do you think he really said that? Will we ultimately rely on preserved tapes of *Entertainment Tonight* or *Hard Copy* to tell us about the entertainment media today? And what do you think it costs to get three minutes of air time on those programs?

That is why the legendary producer Sam Goldwyn used his PR people to build and sustain his reputation as a master of the malaprop. They quoted him with uttering such gems as "Include me out," or "I can answer you in two words—im possible."

I am aware of this phenomenon because it is responsible for my father being ignored in the annals of movie history. He was responsible for more than half of the movies produced by MGM during its first few years of operation in the silent era, but it was studio policy until 1933 not to give a "produced by" credit. If you look at the title cards of MGM movies up to the time that David Selznick was brought in to replace the ailing Irving Thalberg in 1933, you will not find any producer credits at all. There were, in fact, few credits of any kind until the talent guilds and unions demanded screen mention that could lead to financial benefits. This book seeks not only to tell my life story but also to close the "recognition gap" for my father and to explain his important role in the wonderful heyday of MGM.

I hope you feel, as I do, that movies represent a rich cultural heritage and are worth preserving. Despite the inroads of TV and videocassettes which offer, at best, a vicarious substitute for the real thing, movies are still a great medium and going to the movies can still be for most of us one of our most cherished and satisfying cultural experiences. There have been disappointing periods of moviegoing in the past and there will be again—but the best creative talents in the world are attracted to the medium and sooner or later their aspirations will bring about movies of integrity and quality.

That wise comedian Will Rogers used to say that moviegoers were like gold miners: "they just keep going, hoping some day to strike a movie." I've been around long enough to know ~~that~~ he was right—and ~~that~~ just when you give up hope, you strike it rich with something like *Shadowlands, Babe, Il Postino* or *Shall We Dance?* My strike may turn out to be your dry-hole and vice versa, but we will both keep prospecting. That's what makes the movies so wonderful, and that's why I want to tell you what it was like to grow up with them.

August 20, 1998

Chapter 1

My Family

Let me begin by describing the background of my father, movie pioneer Harry Rapf. I do so fully aware that in this day and age, when even movie hairdressers and costume designers can become the subjects of pictorial biographies, my father is a subject worthy of a full-length book. One day my daughter Joanna Rapf, a film professor at the University of Oklahoma, will write the entire story together with an analysis of his very extensive filmography.

My father's early movies—and he branched out from vaudeville to movies in 1916—were sold on a "state rights" basis. That is to say, when a film was finished, my father put the cans under his arm and traveled around to neighboring cities such as Philadelphia, Boston, and Washington, D.C., to make deals for its distribution. He worked in this independent manner until about 1919 when he agreed to be a production manager and to produce for Select Films, which was headed by Lewis J. Selznick and William Brady. The company had offices in Manhattan and production facilities in Fort Lee, New Jersey.

It was at the Selznick studio in Fort Lee that I first met David O. Selznick, who was later to gain considerable fame as the producer of *Gone With The Wind.* He was about seventeen years old at the time, but he wore grown-up suits and a straw hat and drove a big car. Later, I learned that his father, Lewis J. Selznick, gave him an allowance of a thousand dollars a week, a tidy sum for a teenager at any time but astronomical in 1919. The idea, according to L. J., was to get the young man accustomed to having a lot of money so ~~that~~ he would eventually have to make it on his own. (My mother had a similar philosophy, which she tried to pass on as advice to my frugal wife:

1

"Spend," she said. "If you run up a lot of bills, you give your husband the incentive to make money to pay for them.")

My family moved to Hollywood when my father joined the fledgling Warner Bros. company, which had its studio on Sunset Boulevard east of Gower. Here, my father's position was like that of a fifth Warner brother, but he was the most experienced of all of them at turning out movies, and he launched what was to be the studio's biggest moneymaker—the series of films with the dog star Rin Tin Tin (most of them written by a young man from Nebraska named Darryl Zanuck, who would later be the top man at 20th Century–Fox).

Although my father's movies were quite successful, much of the Warner Bros. product was not because as a small studio they had no theaters to guarantee distribution. Consequently they were, at the end of 1923, on the verge of bankruptcy and would have closed down were it not for the largesse of a Los Angeles banker named Motley Flint.

My father, peering into what must have been a clouded crystal ball, saw a dim future for his confreres, the brothers Warner, and he thus accepted an offer from Louis B. Mayer, another small independent, who was in the process of working out a merger (under the aegis of Loews Incorporated) with the much larger Metro company and the Samuel Goldwyn company, which had a large movie production plant in Culver City.

The new company, Metro-Goldwyn-Mayer, was officially launched in April of 1924 with my father, Mayer, and young Irving Thalberg as the triumvirate that was to guide its production destiny and to provide the raw material for the parent Loews Theater chain. My father remained with the company until he died in February 1949 at the age of sixty-seven. His most productive years were in the 1920s, when he was individually responsible for more than half of the approximately forty movies produced by MGM each year. His most prestigious years were from 1929 to 1933, when movies made under his supervision—or writers and actors connected with those movies—won at least five Academy Awards.

The Warner Bros. company, as most everyone knows, rescued itself from bankruptcy a year or so after my father's departure by introducing the first successful use of theater sound on film. It was the Bell Labs' system known as "Vitaphone." The sound was on a disk—a large record which ran at 33⅓ revolutions per minute, with a coordinating cable to the movie projector so that the sound could be synchronized with the projector (except when the needle skipped a groove or the film skipped a couple of frames).

But the addition of sound to the silent screen was more than a novelty; it was a revelation. And within a few years audiences would demand not just synchronized music and sound effects but spoken words emanating from the mouths of their favorite screen personalities. And the Warner brothers were the first to fill this demand.

At first, the use of speech or singing was confined to short subjects and newsreels. Sound was actually introduced in a kind of photographed stage setting with a screened curtain that parted while the head of the Motion Picture Producers and Distributors of America, Will Hays (who had been postmaster general under President Harding), stepped forward and told the audience about the miracle they were about to see. Then there were short subjects: Giovanni Martinelli, a Metropolitan Opera tenor, sang "Vesti La Giuba" from *I Pagliacci;* John Barrymore did the "To Be or Not to Be" speech from *Hamlet;* there were short bits by violinists Efrem Zimbalist and Mischa Elman; a soprano solo, "Caro Nome" from *Rigoletto,* was sung by Marion Talley; and there was another solo by Anna Case and the Cansino dancers. Then came the feature film, John Barrymore in *Don Juan,* with Mary Astor. It was a silent film but had a recorded musical score and sound effects.

I saw this first Warner Bros. sound program at Grauman's Egyptian theatre on Hollywood Boulevard, but it was another film, *The Jazz Singer,* featuring Al Jolson, in 1927, with its synchronous sound dialogue sequences that altered the course of movie history and catapulted Warner Bros. from a poverty-stricken independent to a major Hollywood studio. By 1929, every studio, including MGM, had converted to sound.

MGM's Culver City studio was my father's workplace until he died. It was my playground as I grew up, from 1924 to 1927, and thereafter a place for summer jobs. Ultimately, a year or so after graduation from Dartmouth, it provided my first job as a junior writer in the movie industry.

One question often asked about my father and his role at the studio is just what a producer like him actually does. A simple answer is that under the old studio system, he was the boss. He was expected to produce a certain number of movies each year. For the most part, he chose the story material, he hired the writer or writers to do a screen version of the original material, and he worked with the writers until he was convinced that he had a screenplay that he considered satisfactory for production—usually referred to as "a shooting script." At that point, he sought the most desirable director he could find for the material. In a big studio like MGM his choice was usually limited to an available director under contract—although my father sometimes went off the lot, as he did when he borrowed Mervyn LeRoy from Warner Bros. to do the Dressler-Beery movie *Tugboat Annie*. He would then okay or refuse the changes in the script that were requested by the director and supervise the casting, the budget, the schedule, and every other phase of production preparation.

Once principal photography began, he might or might not make frequent visits to the set, but he definitely reviewed each day's work (the "rushes" or "dailies"), sometimes with the director but always with the editor, with whom he would continue to work when shooting was completed, having the responsibility at that time of assigning composers, musicians, and title and special effects experts to the film.

In this way, the producer was the one person who was responsible for the fate of a movie from its inception to its completion. This required creativity in the writing stages, business acumen in production planning, knowledge of filmmaking skills during production and editing, and marketing savvy when it came to selling the finished product to the public. But the old-time producers like my father and Irving Thalberg did not work alone. They had assistants—most of whom ultimately were to become producers on their own. (Some of my father's early assistants were David Selznick, Jack Cummings, Lou Edelman, Lawrence Weingarten, Frank Davis, and Leonard Spiegelgass.)

In a movie factory like MGM, there were experts to guide a film through specific phases such as research, budget, set design, costuming, music, and the final mixing and lab work. And since the old studios were vertical industries, the completion of a movie activated another set of experts, who worked out advertising and distribution campaigns to the theaters owned by the parent company (Loews Incorporated, in the case of MGM) and independent theaters as well.

By the time my father participated in the founding of MGM, he was very familiar with the ins and outs of show business and had worked for eight years as a movie producer on his own and with others. Although born in New York City in 1881, he was raised in Denver. His father, Maurice, who had emigrated from somewhere in the Austro-Hungarian Empire (probably from what is now known as the Czech Republic), was a successful tailor with a shop on lower Fifth Avenue in New York City. When Maurice contracted tuberculosis, he was ordered to get out of town and to move to a higher clime, to a city with medical facilities that could treat the disease. In those days—around 1890—that was Denver, if you could afford the move. The Rapf family could.

As it turned out, my grandfather Maurice (for whom I am named) died a few years later, leaving his young wife, Eliza, with four sons, the oldest of whom was my father. She had some money but no means of continuing support, so she bought a grocery store ~~that~~ she ran with the help of her children. For a woman who had never worked, it was a gutsy move and her sons remained in awe of her for the rest of their lives. They also felt obligated to see to her well being—and she lived to be eighty-eight.

Why my father was drawn to theatricals and to show business I don't know (with his brains and energy he might have founded a grocery chain), but I am told ~~that~~ he began to stage shows in high school, that some were good enough to get bookings around Denver, and that he haunted the local vaudeville house and tried to duplicate some of the routines he saw there in his own presentations. When he was about twenty-one, having achieved something of a reputation as a Denver impresario, he went backstage to meet a popular vaudevillian, Gus Edwards, who had an act known as *Gus Edwards' School Boys and Girls*. It consisted of a classroom set and a group of precocious youngsters who performed dances, songs, and comic routines under the tutelage of their onstage teacher, Edwards himself.

My father apparently invited the great man to see one of his semi-professional Denver shows. (I think it was in minstrel form.) Edwards liked it and must have liked my father, too, because he offered him a job as the road manager of the school act, a job that my father filled for the next five or six years, most of the time without Edwards taking part in it. Edwards, in addition to performing in the School Boys and Girls act, was also a songwriter of note—the most familiar of his works being the theme song of the vaudeville act, which one still hears from time to time:

> School days, school days—
> dear old golden rule days—
> taught to the tune of the hickory stick . . .

He also wrote "Sunbonnet Sue," "Jimmy Valentine," "In My Merry Oldsmobile," "By the Light of the Silvery Moon," and many others. He was famous as a "Starmaker" (title of a filmed biography starring Bing Crosby in 1939) and was credited with discovering Eleanor

Powell, Ray Bolger, Eddie Cantor, Hildegarde, and others. In later years, when my father was a top gun at MGM and produced its first musical variety show, *The Hollywood Revue of 1929,* he brought Gus Edwards to Hollywood, gave him a featured role in that movie, and let him introduce a few new songs, including "It's Orange Blossom Time" and the sentimental "Your Mother and Mine."

The act my father managed for Edwards proved, as did other Edwards' productions, to be a stepping stone to stardom for precocious kids such as George Jessel, Walter Winchell, Georgie Price, and the delectable child known as "Cuddles," who went into movies as Lila Lee. Edwards' home office secretary in New York City was Clementine Uhlfelder, a straitlaced young German-Jewish lady who had strenuous objections to some of the items sent in by my father as part of the act's expense account. Vitriolic correspondence passed back and forth between the two, but they did not meet for at least three years. My father could not believe that the cute, pretty little girl everyone called "Tina" was the one who had been giving him such a hard time all those years. Nevertheless he asked for a date and they were married in 1911. I was born three years later.

My earliest memories are of a large apartment at 640 Riverside Drive, which is at 141st Street in Manhattan. There was—and still is—a crescent shaped plot of grass between the front of the apartment building and the Drive itself. That plot was often my playground, and I recall being hit by a car and tossed over the fence while crossing from the crescent to the apartment without looking either way. I think I was in the first grade at P.S. 186 (on 145th Street between Broadway and Amsterdam) at the time, because I remember being pleased that the accident—which caused no great pain—would keep me out of school for a few days.

The other activity I remember well is acting in my father's movies. He had a penchant for movies about youngsters, and as an "extra" and occasional bit player I came cheap. Besides, he was a very doting father and liked to take me with him whenever he went on location, whether I was appearing before the cameras or not. And since I didn't start school until 1920, there were several preschool years in which I went off to work with my father several times a week.

In 1920 or thereabouts, he started making a series of pictures with a freckle-faced child star named Wesley Barry. He starred Barry in a film called *School Days,* with appropriate credit to his mentor and first employer, Gus Edwards. I was used as an extra in a poverty-stricken country schoolroom and again in the fancy city school where Barry went when he was adopted by rich city folk. There is a still photograph (which appears later in this book) from a Rapf-produced Barry melodrama in which I am the boy in the Norfolk jacket being threatened by a bully.

When an offer came from Warner Bros. in 1920, the whole family went to the West Coast for a look-see, and the family included my grandmother, my father's mother, Eliza. Grandma Rapf was, in fact, a permanent part of our household until she died shortly after World War II. As I was often told—by relatives who found this hard to believe—when my father proposed marriage to my mother, he made it clear that his mother would be part of the deal. In other words, "Take me, take my mother."

Just why Tina accepted this onerous condition I never knew, but she had a mother-in-law in her household until the old lady died. There were, to be sure, some advantages to this otherwise uncomfortable arrangement. There were also some serious psychological drawbacks. My grandmother planned all the meals and did the shopping. She taught a succession of cooks how to make pot roast and potato pancakes and lemon meringue pie and all of the other dishes that my father liked, and she never went out at night so she was a permanent baby-sitter. But she ruled the house, just as she continued to rule my father as if he were still in knee pants. I can remember—when he was in his fifties—that she would point a finger at him from her place at the head of the table and say, "Eat your spinach, Harry—it's good for you." And he would obey.

It was Grandma Rapf who gave the final okay to our West Coast move, even though the 1920 visit resulted in severe cases of pneumonia for her and my mother. The pneumomia led to an enforced stay in Palm Springs, then something of a frontier village with a healthy climate (and cowboys on horses who scared the hell out of me).

Grandma was a smart old lady and she knew that the future of the motion picture business was in Hollywood, not in New York. So my father took the job with Warner Bros., we went back to New York at the end of summer, my mother gave birth to my brother Matthew in October, and then we made the big move, arriving in Los Angeles on May 19, 1921—my seventh birthday.

One of my father's younger brothers, Joe, had married a Los Angeles girl and now ran her parents' dress shop downtown on Broadway near Third Street. (Joe was said to be a "cloak and suiter," whatever that means.) His wife, Vera (a dead ringer for Margaret Hamilton, the noted witch of *The Wizard of Oz*), had rented an apartment for us in a new building, the Lafayette Arms, near Wilshire and across from Lafayette Park. Vera came from a fine old Jewish family named Feintuch, and I remember her parents especially for the elegant electric car they drove and the fancy flower vase that graced the back seat.

Living near Lafayette Park (which is still there), I was hustled off to the Hoover Street Elementary School for the balance of the school year, and, because my parents were constantly on the move during the next few years (always renting but hoping to find a permanent abode) I sampled a good many elementary schools in the area between Union Street and Crenshaw Boulevard. In addition to the Hoover Street School, there was Union, Cahuenga, and Wilton Place, the school I entered in the third grade when my parents finally settled on a home of their own at 621 Lorraine Boulevard, part of a section known then as Windsor Square.

Our first rentals—near Lafayette Park, on Rampart Street, on 6th and Union, and on Mariposa (near the Ambassador Hotel)— had all been south of, but not too far from, Warner Bros. My parents did not, however, buy the house on Lorraine until my father was ensconced at MGM in Culver City, a good twenty minutes to the southwest. And there my family remained until World War II, when—with their two sons no longer at home and servants difficult to find—they decided to sell the house and move into a series of furnished apartments that provided basic services. They were living in an apartment at the Beverly Wilshire Hotel when my grandmother died in 1946.

They subsequently moved to an apartment complex owned by Joan Crawford on South Rodeo Drive in Beverly Hills, and some wags thought that this was to accommodate my mother, an inveterate shopper, because it was within walking distance of Saks Fifth Avenue on Wilshire Boulevard where she spent most of her days (no doubt "spending" to keep her husband ambitious).

I should mention here one positive aspect of my father's career that is frequently alluded to in books about the movies: the fact that he discovered Joan Crawford. Miss Crawford's own autobiography tells the story of his seeing her dancing in a New York night club, inviting her for a screen test, and subsequently giving her a contract to come to Hollywood. I think I met Joan the first day she arrived at the studio. She was sixteen at the time and I was eleven, but that didn't stop me from fantasizing a relationship with her. She was a bit plump, with a face that was much rounder than the one we are familiar with, and the famous Crawford eyes had not yet exploded into those big saucers ~~that~~ we know so well. (Some people claimed it took an operation to accomplish that.) But she was a very attractive girl. The result was that even though I had always spent a lot of time at the studio, usually taking a friend who could join me in some imaginary adventure, using whatever sets were available, I now bugged my father to take me with him every Saturday and I sometimes preferred to go without any friends at all.

Joan's name was actually Lucille Le Seur, but the studio didn't think that would look good on a marquee. They advertised a contest in fan magazines with a $500 prize to go to the person sending in the best new name for this promising starlet. The name they selected was "Joan Arden." (Somewhere, I have a picture that was autographed during the short period when she was Joan Arden—"To the sweetest little boy in the world"—an affectionate thought but not exactly a desirable inscription for a teenager with a crush on her.) Well, it turned out that two people had submitted the "Joan Arden" name and the ad had said, "Equal prizes in case of a tie." So, as I recall the incident (and Crawford herself tells a different story in her autobiography, but I think I'm right), the studio concluded that paying two prizes was ridiculous and they made up their own name, "Crawford," and gave no prize at all.

My father was noted for his skill in spotting talent and, despite having a rather crusty exterior, for being a soft touch when it came to giving newcomers a chance, whether actors, directors, or writers. Several of my college friends got their first jobs as junior writers because of my father's largesse. And people I knew well told me that the reason he started the MGM shorts department—though it was obviously intended for profit—was as a breeding ground for new talent (and a haven for otherwise unemployable relatives).

One old friend, Dick Goldstone, who was hired out of UCLA by my father, later headed the shorts department. He wrote a book—as yet unpublished—in which he makes it clear that even when my father was merely overseeing the running of the department, he kept close tabs on newcomers and frequently gave them their first chance at making features. He would also call other producers' attention to new talent, as he did to Robert Taylor, whose first acting job at MGM was in a *Crime Does Not Pay* short.

It is also true that he used the shorts department and other areas of the studio to provide jobs for some of his indigent relatives. I re-

member him giving hell to the head of the casting office for not calling a distant cousin on a day when they were using hundreds of five-
dollar extras in a mob scene.

Not all of the relatives remained indigent, however. My father invited his favorite cousin, Minnie Katz, to come to the coast with her
sixteen-year-old son Raymond to spend the summer in their Malibu
beach house. While in California, young Raymond persuaded my father to give him his first job. It was in the MGM mail room, and
when cousin Minnie returned to New York, Raymond stayed on to
live with the Rapfs on Lorraine Boulevard.

Like so many other young men, Raymond found the pretty young
starlets hard to resist. According to his testimony, he established a
chaste relationship with Dixie Dean, Jean Harlow's "stand-in." Since
he lived with my parents but had no car, Dixie picked him up every day
and drove him to and from the studio, where she was under contract.
One day Dixie stopped by my father's office at the studio. The reason?
She said she was pregnant and that Raymond was the father but would-
n't marry her. She asked for a new MGM contract that would not require her to be Harlow's stand-in or she would create a scandal.

My father, the MGM mogul, told her not to worry. He would see
to it that justice was done. But his idea of justice was to chastise Raymond and to send him packing back to New York on the next train.
Dixie Dean worked at the studio until it was time for the studio to
pick up her next option. It turned out there was no baby, and as a result the option was not picked up.

We never heard of her again. Raymond, on the other hand, went
to work as assistant stage manager at the famous Capitol Theater in
New York City under the aegis of L. K. Sidney (father of director
George Sidney). Within six months (Raymond was seventeen at the
time) he was promoted to stage manager, later to be program director of the MGM radio station, WHN. When MGM, under the
government's consent decree, sold the radio station as well as the
Loew Theaters, Raymond resigned to devote himself full-time to the
personal management business. Today, he is one of the premier
managers in the entertainment world whose clients have included
Lily Tomlin, Whoopi Goldberg, Melissa Gilbert, Joan Rivers,
Richard Pryor, Dolly Parton, Anthony Newley, Steve Guttenberg,
and others.

Raymond's mother, Minnie, lived with him until she died in 1984
at the age of ninety-four. Minnie was the daughter of Grandma Rapf's

brother and therefore was my father's first cousin. It was said that Harry Rapf looked out for Minnie as if she were indeed the little sister he never had. He had to approve of any young man who dared to date her. She ultimately married a millinery manufacturer and salesman, and when ladies' hats went out of style, so did his rather successful business. Son Raymond more than made up for the millinery losses, but he is the first to admit ~~that~~ it was the beneficent family influence that got him started.

(My father was not alone in practicing nepotism. It was said that Carl Laemmle, founder and head of Universal Pictures, made many trips to Europe, usually to take the baths at Bad Nauheim, and he always came back with relatives who became known as "Laemmle's foreign legion." When he died, more than seventy relatives or close friends were found on the Universal payroll, including two men who were dead.)

During the course of his career, my father, like other movie moguls, had various summer homes. The first one I remember was on the oceanfront in Santa Monica within walking distance of L. B. Mayer's, Irving Thalberg's, and Jack Warner's homes. The twelve- or fourteen-room house we rented was actually on property owned by William Randolph Hearst. It was a guest house for the huge hotel-like establishment, complete with Olympic-size swimming pool, that he had built for his lady-love, the actress Marion Davies. (That white-pillared structure still stands, but it has been converted to a fancy beach club.)

I know ~~that~~ we rented the Davies-Hearst guest house for the summer of 1928 because that was the year ~~when~~ I got my first driver's license (at age fourteen in California in those days) and, shortly thereafter, my first automobile. Thomas, our chauffeur, taught me how to drive in my parents' Cadillac limousine, which, without synchro-mesh transmission, was not an easy car for shifting gears. Since it was about three feet longer than the average car, parking was no cinch, either. Once I could manage the limo, taking the driving test in my father's Buick coupe was a snap. And, with license in the offing and after much wheedling on my part, my parents promised me a car of my own for my fourteenth birthday. I had assured them I could find something fairly cheap, probably for less than a hundred dollars, and I started reading the classified ads and making a tour of the used car lots.

Believe it or not, there were many cars advertised for less than one hundred dollars in those days, including venerable Ford Model T's that would require my learning new skills in order to shift gears with a foot pedal. Ford no longer manufactured the Model T, having launched a four cylinder Model A with the gas tank in front of the windshield. Well, I found a car; I think it was a 1924 Dodge, sometimes called a "Dodgé," as if it were French, and I took my father to see it one Saturday afternoon. He took one look and shook his head. "I can't let you drive that heap," he said. "It's dangerous. How much would a new car cost?"

So I went to the local Ford and Chevrolet dealers and found ~~that~~ it was possible to buy a new Chevrolet roadster for four hundred and seventy-five dollars. It was actually a bit more than that because the quoted price didn't include a spare wheel with a tire. You picked your brand in those days—-Goodrich, Firestone, Goodyear, or Kelly-Springfield (the latter had a wonderful print ad that featured a small boy in long johns with a tire over his shoulder and the caption "Time to Retire"). The spare tire added about twenty-five dollars to the cost. Later, you would buy an automatic windshield wiper, wind wings, and a fancy ornament that included a thermometer to replace the prosaic radiator cap on the front of the hood. So much for that first vehicle, which I drove with pride from the beachfront of Santa Monica to L. A. High School for several weeks from mid-May to the end of June and during summer vacation.

Our rented beach house was so spacious that we were invaded by family visitors from the East. My mother was always big on relatives, and my father and grandmother threw out the welcome mat for anyone who came from Denver, where they had spent the last years of the nineteenth century. That summer, I remember visits from a large contingent of New York Uhlfelders (my mother's family, including my grandparents, a few uncles and cousins), Herbie Stein and Blanche Preeman from Denver, and the Newmans, former Denver residents now operating theaters in Seattle. The Newmans' daughter Vi became the first wife of Pandro Berman, later a noted movie producer.

That Fourth of July, my friend Budd Schulberg and I pooled our resources to buy fireworks in Culver City, where their sale was legal, and we worked out a program and set up chairs for our parents and friends to watch our display on the Santa Monica beachfront as soon as it got dark. We had begun with a modest overture of a few sparklers and roman candles when suddenly we heard a loud bang in the sky and, in a moment, we could see explosives form a huge American flag. And there, down the beach, in front of the Davies estate, was a cannon that had catapulted this elaborate fireworks display into the sky. And that was just the beginning. Every fifteen seconds or so, another monster display burst in the sky above our heads. The puny sky rockets we had prepared, the pinwheels and flaming fountains, would have to wait for another occasion. All eyes were obviously on the Hearst-Davies fountain of lights down the beach. As Budd said, "Davies shooting off *her* stuff made *our* stuff look sick."

In 1929, my parents actually built a second home in the Malibu beach colony—an area that then was and still is a haven for people in the entertainment industry. The Malibu land was owned in 1929 by the scion of a pioneer California family, Mrs. Rindge, who refused to sell. But she needed money after the stock market crash, so at the end of the 1920s she decided to lease the beachfront land in thirty-foot parcels on a ten-year basis, at a dollar a front foot, to those who chose to build on it and were willing to take the risk that she might not renew the leases at the end of ten years. (This accounts for the fact that to this day so many of the houses in the Malibu colony nearly abut each other and are built, for the most part, on narrow lots at right angles to the ocean.)

My parents built a twelve-room house on their thirty feet and then leased another ten feet to the north which made that side of the house more open than most of the others. Rosabelle, the daughter of Carl Laemmle, president and founder of Universal, built on the lot directly south of us. She had once been engaged to Irving Thalberg, who jilted her to marry Norma Shearer, causing her to be known as "Poor Rosabelle." But Poor Rosabelle rebounded quickly, married a nice chap named Stanley Bergerman (later to become a successful agent), and then built their beach house so close to ours that we could touch hands if we reached out of our respective bedroom windows.

Some of the happiest years of my life were spent at Malibu. My father, an avid fisherman, chartered a fishing boat almost every Saturday during the summers and would take off from the Malibu pier with his cronies (Leon Schlesinger of Looney Tunes and Bill Koenig, general manager of Universal, were habitués) to catch barracuda, yellowtail, and the staple of the kelp bed area, calico bass, some of which ran as large as five pounds.

My close friend Budd Schulberg, son of B. P. Schulberg, then the production chief at Paramount (whose family had built on ninety feet of Mrs. Rindge's land), usually went along on these fishing trips. He and I earned our right of passage by cleaning everyone's fish, then taking what the fishermen didn't want to distribute to our adult movie friends along the Malibu beach—such people as the directors Herbert

Brenon, Frank Capra, Bob Leonard, and Tod Browning; the actors Neil Hamilton, Maureen O'Sullivan, Ruth Chatterton, and Ralph Forbes; and various producers, writers, and agents. Our rewards might be delicious milkshakes at the Brenon's living room soda fountain or a sail with O'Sullivan's boyfriend and later husband, John Farrow. It was fun.

On Sundays, most Malibu residents had open houses, which is to say that there were a few invited guests and many more who knew they would not be turned away. (The Schulbergs had a tennis court that was a special attraction.) After a while, my mother began to dread these Sunday invasions, but it was my grandmother who supervised the preparation of the food—her pot roast (made from the brisket) and potato pancakes achieving considerable fame and often attracting too many guests.

I was always puzzled by the fact that the "movie crowd" often left the temperate Los Angeles area on weekends, despite the fact that they lived suburban lives with tennis courts, swimming pools, and easy access to the beach—especially after the founding of the Malibu colony, which had been preceded by the popularity of the ocean front in Santa Monica. But there were frequent weekend jaunts—to Palm Springs, to the Coronado Beach Hotel, to Agua Caliente during its short period of existence, to Arrowhead Springs, to Big Bear, to Santa Barbara, even as far north as to Carmel and Monterey. (Bear in mind that in the 1920s and early 1930s, Las Vegas, though it already had legalized gambling, was a rough and tumble frontier town, used by Hollywood folk primarily for quick marriages and divorces.) I suppose that since most movie people were transplanted easterners, they were accustomed to escaping from the workplace to the countryside. And those weekend jaunts were usually taken by groups of intimate friends—mostly movie people, to be sure, but crossing studio lines.

One cohesive group that would turn up in Coronado, or Palm Springs, or Arrowhead was what we called "the British crowd"—with the veteran character actor C. Aubrey Smith as the doyen of this cricket-playing group, which consisted of Ronald Colman and his wife, Benita Hume, Basil and Ouida Rathbone, Ruth Chatterton and Ralph Forbes, Brian Aherne, Cedric Hardwicke, and others. The industry was largely controlled by Hollywood's Jewish moguls, but the British "colony" was singularly immune to integration with the bosses. The bosses, in turn, seemed to be somewhat in awe of the snooty Britishers. One can see how this is reflected in many films of the thirties (*The Charge of the Light Brigade, Gunga Din, Beau Geste,*

Four Feathers, Lives of a Bengal Lancer) in which the superiority and stiff upper lip of British colonialism is dramatized (and many British actors are employed). Norman Zierold, a Jewish literary critic, wrote of what he described as "our crowd on the West Coast. . . . They were conducting a gentile art form, selling the blonde hair and blue eyes of Mary Pickford. 'The movie moguls,' as they were called, tended to divest themselves of their Jewishness. They dealt in talent and it bore no trace of race or nationality."

One can't really talk sensibly about Hollywood and how it flourished without talking about the Jews who crossed the continent to be its pioneers and were to sit on the thrones of its major companies for the next forty years. I feel qualified to write on this subject since my father, Harry Rapf, was one of those Jewish pioneers.

It is not particularly well-known that the whole phenomenon of Hollywood was an accident, perpetrated by Jews. Consider that one producer, Jesse Lasky, went west in 1913 to get out from under the severe restrictions of Thomas Edison's non-Jewish Motion Picture Patents Company, which would license but not sell the necessary equipment for making and showing movies. It was Lasky's intention to set up production facilities in Flagstaff, Arizona, which was said to have a temperate climate and was near the Mexican border, over which it was his plan to import new equipment from Europe. Yet because he ran into one of Flagstaff's rare periods of continuous rain, he moved on, after several days of frustration, to Los Angeles where the weather was perfect. He then wired back to his partner, Sam Goldwyn (then Goldfish): "Want permission to rent barn in a place called Hollywood for $75 a month."

Well, although my father was certainly a pioneer, he didn't take his family west until seven years after Lasky's jaunt. My father went west because making movies was his business and that's where the action was. Like the other Jewish pioneers, he wanted to make movies and he wanted to make money. Fortunately, he did both. But what always seemed extraordinary to me is that my father's business (and it was just that) should have survived and flourished, not only as a business but as the subject of so much serious and scholarly attention. As a result, when Dartmouth gives me the opportunity to teach film or when I write these words, I am given the enviable opportunity of paying homage to my family heritage.

People do often ask the question, "Are movies a Jewish industry?" The answer is, for the most part, "Yes." And, for some reason ~~that~~ I can't hope to explain, there are to this day more Jews holding positions of prominence in the film industry than in any other industry except perhaps the garment trade. And there have been times (the present being no exception) that if it features even isolated examples of subject matter inimical to the conservative establishment the industry has been attacked (as have its media related cousins, TV and the press) with veiled and even blatant anti-Semitism.

This was particularly noticeable in the period between 1939 and 1941 when a few pro-British and antifascist films were made, and some of the leaders of the isolationist America First movement pointed an accusing finger at the movie industry leaders as being warmongers. Senator Burton K. Wheeler said, "An industry controlled by foreign-born producers persists in making pictures calculated to dragging the U.S. into war." And Charles Lindbergh, the famed "Lone Eagle" and the first man to make a solo plane crossing of the Atlantic, who was also an America Firster, said, "Jews are particularly dangerous because of their ownership and influence in movies, the press, radio and the government."

When some Hollywood people attacked the investigation into the communist influence in movies by the House Un-American Activities Committee, a Southern congressman, John Rankin, read the names of this liberal opposition into the *Congressional Record* as follows: "Danny Kaye, and we found his real name was David Daniel Kaminski . . . Another one is Eddie Cantor, whose real name is Edward Iskowitz . . . There is one who calls himself Edward Robinson. His real name is Emanuel Goldenberg." Rankin reeled off the names of others in the same vein. Those named were, he said, "attacking the committee for doing its duty in trying to protect this country and save the American people from the horrible fate the Communists have meted out to the unfortunate Christian people of Europe."

If the truth was that industry policy was in Jewish hands, it was also true that these hands belonged to hard-nosed businessmen who had risen, in a sense, from rags to riches and—with the rarest of exceptions, such as with my friend and sponsor, Walter Wanger—they could be expected to line up on the conservative side of any political issue.

Let's go back a little to note the origins of Jewish control: Adolph Zukor, who had imported a full-length feature starring Sarah Bernhardt and had a contract with "America's Sweetheart," Mary Pickford, founded Famous Players, later joining hands with Jesse Lasky to head Paramount. A mite-sized German immigrant, Carl Laemmle, headed

Universal; Marcus Loew, Nicholas Schenck, and Louis B. Mayer controlled MGM; William Fox headed the studio bearing his name, as did the Warner brothers, who absorbed First National and moved their headquarters from Sunset Boulevard to Burbank. The Cohn brothers' company was Columbia, with Harry running production in Hollywood and his brother Jack handling distribution from the New York office. The major independents were Samuel Goldwyn, Charlie Chaplin, David Selznick, Sol Lesser, and Edward Small. Indeed, the only major studio not founded and run by Jews was RKO, formerly FBO, where there were a variety of top dogs during the twenties and early thirties, including Joseph Kennedy, father of a man who would some day be president of the United States. But the heads of production from 1934 until 1950, when Howard Hughes took over RKO, were David Selznick, Pandro Berman and Dore Schary—all Jews.

Most of these men were immigrants or children of immigrants, imbued with the idea that the United States was a land of opportunity. (To give you an idea of their humble origins, Goldwyn was a glove salesman, Zukor a furrier, the Warners worked in their father's butcher shop, Mayer was a junk dealer in Nova Scotia, and so forth.) These men came from families that observed the Jewish religious traditions, but in Hollywood the only suitable Jewish congregation was the reformed B'nai Brith in downtown Los Angeles, with the suave Edgar F. Magnin as rabbi.

I remember being driven in a variety of limousines to B'nai Brith at 9th and Hope in downtown L.A. every Sunday, usually with fellow passengers who were also offspring of Jewish producers: my friend Budd Schulberg, Doris Warner (daughter of Harry and later married to Mervyn LeRoy), Julian Lesser (son of Sol, producer of the Jackie Coogan movies), and John Rogers (son of Charles R., an independent who would later head Universal).

It wasn't until 1930 that a new and resplendent temple was built farther west on Wilshire Boulevard, where the Jewish moguls could attend the High Holy Days in style and be given funeral eulogies by Georgie Jessel in the proper flowered surroundings, with movie fans lined up on either side of the entrance as if they had come to a premiere instead of to a mournful farewell. The best line I know about a B'nai Brith funeral is attributed to producer Sam Goldwyn, who, on seeing the large turnout for the funeral of his not-very-popular rival, Louis B. Mayer, said, "The reason so many people showed up was to make sure he was dead."

These Jewish movie moguls were a much-maligned group of men, with some of the calumny justified, but with much of it showing no appreciation for their dedication to the complex and demanding job of turning out entertainment. For example, the highbrow critic Edmund Wilson wrote in the late 1930s, "It is plain that today's producers, including the Great Goldwyn and the late Irving Thalberg, are the same megalomaniac cloak and suit dealers that their predecessors were. You only have to look at their products."

It was easy for a man like Goldwyn to become the target of intellectuals. Despite the high quality of many of his films (*Dodsworth, These Three, Dead End*) he allowed his publicity people to circulate stories featuring his abuse of the English language with such infamous phrases as "include me out," and "our comedies are not to be laughed at." Even if he didn't say these things, he certainly approved what his press agents made up.

U.S. author, John Dos Passos, in one of his newsreel-like introductions to a chapter in *The 42nd Parallel* wrote:

> Many years ago there lived in a crowded slum in a city under the leaden skies of eastern Europe a little Jewish boy named Samuel. It was a city full of mud and misery. The police wore heavy high leather boots just for the purpose of kicking poor little boys and especially poor little Jewish boys around. The little boy was very skinny and very weak, but there burned in his heart so great an ambition that he decided he'd run away far to the west beyond the Rhine and across the ocean. There was a country called America. "What did I know about it," he says today. "It was a dream."

And despite Edmund Wilson and his ilk, young Samuel (later to be known as Goldwyn) fulfilled the promise of that dream with a product we will continue to look at with pleasure for years to come. Try watching *Wuthering Heights, The Best Years of Our Lives,* and *The Little Foxes,* and you'll know what I mean.

The question then is: Did the fact that the Jews ran the industry have any effect on the way Jews were treated in movies? The answer is "yes, indeed." The reality is that from the early 1930s to the end of World War II, they pretty much weren't dealt with at all. I write about this from firsthand knowledge because my father, though not a devoutly religious man, was not only very proud and extremely conscious of his Jewish heritage but was also annoyed and openly critical of friends who tried to forget where they came from. I have tried to compile his filmography, and I know that some of his earliest films—which I have never seen although I know I was used as a child actor on a few occasions—dealt with Jewish themes. He had spent many years in vaudeville, where ethnic comedians and even ethnic dramatic performers were popular. These people—many of them from the Yiddish theater— had been his clients and friends, and when he started making movies he wanted to use them. I know that he made a number of movies with Vera Gordon, who had been a big star of the Yiddish theater in New York City, and with Bertha Kalish who was a monologist reading Yiddish stories in English on the vaudeville circuit.

Came the thirties and the rise of anti-Semitism in Europe and a national Jewish organization, the Anti-Defamation League, called a meeting of producers in Hollywood, urging them henceforth to switch to a low-profile stance as far as Jewish subjects were concerned, to eliminate Jewish characters (good or bad), and to avoid subjects in which Jewish issues might be raised. Noted Jewish actors such as George Sidney, Rudolph Schildkraut, Sammy Cohen, Benny Rubin, and George E. Stone were henceforth unemployable unless they could play Greeks or Italians. My father had brought the noted Jewish vaudevillians Weber and Fields to Hollywood to do a film and had to cancel it. He had also bought the movie rights to *Nize Baby*, artist and writer Milt Gross's best-seller with comic drawings and dialect about a Jewish family. He brought Gross to Hollywood to work on the screenplay, but that, too, ended up on the shelf.

Rudolph Schildkraut and his son Joseph had come to Hollywood from the Yiddish theater in New York—as did Paul Muni, one of the biggest stars of the thirties in non-Jewish roles. George Arliss played two very famous Jewish characters in his gallery of biographical portraits in the early thirties—Disraeli and the chief honcho of the family in *The House of Rothschild*. But the last film from the thirties that I remember that dealt with a Jewish character in a leading role was Warner Bros'. *The Life of Emile Zola* in 1936. The part of Colonel Dreyfuss—whose trial for alleged treason activates Zola and provides the climax—was in fact played by the well-known Jewish actor Joseph Schildkraut, who continued to play leading roles but never again as a Jew until he appeared as the father in *The Diary of Anne Frank* more than twenty years later. And it is interesting that in dealing with the infamous Dreyfuss affair, there is only one indication of the fact that Dreyfuss was a Jew and that appears in an insert of his military record.

One could miss the whole implication of anti-Semitism if you happened not to see that one line among many: "Religion—Jew."

Here we were in a period when anti-Semitism, as a matter of national policy, was running rampant over Europe. And the Jewish movie industry, with its world-wide influence, decided not only to abandon Jews as characters—whether they are funny, sympathetic, or evil—but not to make any effort at all to combat anti-Semitism on the screen.

It is worth noting that while Jewish subjects were being eliminated, the Irish as an ethnic group were getting a great deal of attention, most of it very favorable. It was almost as if the Jewish producers, having abandoned any defense of their own, were leaning over backwards to appease and please the Irish Catholics of the Legion of Decency, who were largely responsible for putting the industry in a censored straitjacket.

Anti-Defamation League policy had always been to urge a low profile, whereas others—certainly young Jews like me—wanted to see Jewish accomplishment extolled as it was many years later in Abba Eban's PBS TV series, *The Jews*. My heroes in the old days were Jewish athletes—the lightweight boxing champion Benny Leonard; the occasional baseball stars such as Hank Greenberg, Al Rosen, and later Sandy Koufax; the Michigan football player Benny Friedman; and then there was Einstein and Irving Berlin and even Lauren Bacall to boast about.

Jewish heroes and Jewish problems just weren't to be handled on the screen until World War II had ended. Then we had the recognition of the Jewish homeland in Israel and, on the screen, *Gentlemen's Agreement*, *Crossfire*, and *The Men*. Even then there was opposition. When Darryl Zanuck of 20th Century–Fox bought Laura Hobson's *Gentlemen's Agreement*, which was an attack on anti-Semitism, the vigilant industry leader L. B. Mayer brought pressure to cancel its production. "Why get into it?" he said. "We're doing all right." (Years earlier, Mayer had tried to reimburse RKO for the production of *Citizen Kane* to prevent its release, which he was sure would turn William Randolph Hearst against the movie industry. He failed and, although Hearst papers refused advertising for the picture, it was rumored that the publisher was actually somewhat flattered by Welles's film portrait of him.)

Though modern movies reflect a more enlightened view of Jews and other oppressed groups, it is probably still true that the easiest way not to offend any group is to make your villains unemployed white males of Protestant descent from a mythical country like Fredonia (the mythical kingdom of the Marx Brothers' *Duck Soup*).

Jews have risen to positions of great prominence in other media—in the press, in radio and on TV, in the theater, in comic strips, and in the arts of sculpture and painting. What is unique about their role in movies is that they did not just enter an established field and adapt themselves to it—they actually played a major role in creating it.

In *The Jazz Singer*, which ushered in the era of talking pictures, Al Jolson faces the choice of opening in a Broadway musical or replacing his sick father as cantor to sing *Kol Nidre* in the *shul* on Yom Kippur, the holiest day of the Jewish year. As it turns out, he manages to do both successfully, thus bridging the gap between his heritage and the popular culture of his time. And when his mother hears him sing "Mammy" in the Broadway theater, she says, with both pride and sadness, "He isn't my boy anymore. He belongs to the world." And so it was with the pioneers of the movie industry, men like my father. They were Jews—and remained so—but they created a non-Jewish culture that belonged to the world.

Now for a few words about myself.

Chapter 2

My Adolescence

My father had the rather sensible notion that I should learn the movie business from the ground up in order to prepare myself for an executive job at MGM. And since he was a vice president of the most successful movie company in the business, it was easy for him to dictate to a department head that his son be hired for a summer job. This started in 1925 when I was eleven. I became an office boy; one of my principal tasks—in addition to delivering mail (which is shown later in this book in the publicity picture with Norma Shearer)—was taking visitors on tours of the studio. Since the studio was my playground I knew every nook and cranny of it. I was also on good terms with most of the assistant directors and they knew that I was the boss's son, so I had an unfair advantage over the other office guides; I could get my tourists onto "closed" sets to see movies that were actually being made. (On all of the sets but Garbo's. I never could crack them—in silent days or later, when the whole process changed for sound.)

I once took a hundred midshipmen on a tour of the back lot, and the officer in charge offered me a sizeable tip. These offers were not unusual, but accepting them was against the rules. As the boss's son, I followed the rules scrupulously—except when I took the proprietors of a nearby ice cream parlor on a tour and they told me to drop in any time for free sodas, malts, and sundaes. I even let my friends take advantage of that offer.

I graduated from L. A. High School in the winter of 1931. My father expected me to take another job at the studio before matriculating at Stanford University in the fall. But I wanted to break the mold, to get away from Hollywood, to do something exotic, perhaps to sail as a cabin boy on one of the Pacific liners going back and forth from San Pedro, the L. A. port, to Honolulu.

My father had a lot of influence but it couldn't land me a job with the Matson line; his influence, however, *did* get me a sea-going job on a movie crew, shooting background material aboard the aircraft carrier *Saratoga* for a forthcoming feature, *Hell Divers* (released in 1932 and starring Wallace Beery, Clark Gable, and Conrad Nagel). I was totally inexperienced, of course, but my assignment was as the third man on the sound crew, which consisted of a recordist, a mixer, and me—who handled the cables and microphone. There were three first cameramen, each with an assistant, and our supervisor and liaison with the Navy, Retired Commander Frank "Spig" Weade, who was also to be the writer of the as-yet-incomplete screenplay. Spig was retired from the Navy when he lost the use of his legs by falling down an elevator shaft (it was said that he was drunk) and he subsequently became a successful writer of screen stories. In addition to my work with the sound crew, I retyped his pages and oiled the squeaky hinges on his leg braces.

The *Saratoga* was heading from San Pedro to Panama to take part in maneuvers for the defense of the Panama Canal. The film crew's objective was to get background footage—mostly airplane takeoffs and landings—to be used in the movie, about which little was known except that the action would take place during those maneuvers. Recording sound with picture was at this point a relatively new operation. Even though radio had been manufacturing believable sound effects for years, the studios, new to the sound medium, were obsessed with obtaining *authentic* sound effects. Hence, our sound crew was to get the bona fide airplane motor noises and, subsequently, the sounds of traffic and street noise in Panama City.

This was before the introduction of magnetic film and tape, so our equipment was huge and bulky. Sound recording was done optically on film with a camera that could transform sound waves into vibrations of light. Our principal recorder, which contained the electronic amplifiers and the camera, was housed in a box about the size of a coffin; it weighed several hundred pounds. Most of the sound aboard ship was recorded in synchronization with the cameras that were shooting takeoffs and landings from the deck of the aircraft carrier.

There were nets jutting out from the overhang of the flight decks on both port and starboard sides. My job was to lie in the net at the starboard bow, holding a microphone to record the sound of a plane taking off over my head. In Panama City, the recording equipment was installed in the back of a truck and I sat on the hood, holding the mike, while we drove through the city recording street noise.

Although our recordings—aboard ship and in the streets—were totally unnecessary and were probably never used in the final film, it was a fabulous trip and much more exotic than anything I might have experienced on a liner to Honolulu. For one thing, we were aboard as observers when the *Saratoga* took the lead as part of the "blue" fleet defending the Panama Canal against the invading "red" fleet. We had an admiral aboard (his name was Reeves) who gathered the ship's crew on the flight deck each night and gave a rundown of the day's simulated battle. On the third day, he announced that we had been sunk by enemy bombers. In point of fact, we did indeed nearly lose some of our own bombers, which ran out of fuel before they could land on deck and thus took a dive into the drink.

Once out of the battle, we put into a bay (Bahía Honda) in Costa Rica and went swimming and fishing and exploring the villages in the jungle despite the presence of huge manta rays in the water between the ship and shore. Then came the farewell party in Panama City for the enlisted men who had helped us aboard ship. It started in a sa-loon, where one of the objectives of the gobs and the film crew was to get me drunk. Not easy, since—at sixteen—I didn't like beer, whiskey, or gin. But I did nibble on the pretzels, anchovies, and salty hors d'oeuvres and I did get thirsty and when there was no Coca Cola available, I found the beer an acceptable substitute to ease my thirst.

How much I drank I don't know. What I do know is that I found myself hours later standing in the back of a carametta (a horse-drawn carriage) delivering speeches in English to the Spanish-speaking pop-ulace, and when we returned to our hotel on the central square, I barely made it to the room, dashed across to the balcony, and tossed up all those salty hors d'oeuvres and beer into the street below. When I "came to" the next day with a terrible hangover, I was told that be-fore the debacles in the carametta and on the hotel balcony we had visited the red light district where, because I was having my first bona fide drunk, I was also introduced to another "first." To this day, I don't know whether that's true or not, but I did allow myself to be taken to the Navy prophylactorium to have the necessary "shot" to protect me from a possible infection.

This was not really my first disastrous bout with alcohol, nor would it be my last. My first "drunk" occurred when I was twelve, following a

Passover seder dinner in my parents' home where my friend Budd Schulberg and I were given grape juice instead of Manischewitz holiday wine as the blessed "fruit of the vine." Remember that this Passover occurred during Prohibition. I happened to know that the gallon jug of holiday wine was hidden in a hall closet. At least half of it was untouched until Schulberg and I went at it—after *Had Gad Ya* ("An Only Kid") had been sung and dinner ended. The result—fearsome intoxication and nasty hangovers, leading us both to make a solemn commitment never to drink alcohol again. The commitment lasted for two years and ended one night at the Schulbergs' when we came across a full bottle of Cointreau—a sweet liquor that is easy on the palate but even more potent than the Manischewitz and with similar results, which led to another two year oath of abstention. I swore a similar oath after the devastating incident in Panama, but that didn't last two years. I went to Panama in January 1931 and entered Stanford as a freshman in the fall.

My father knew something about the boozy proclivities of college students, especially in those days of Prohibition when drinking was enticingly illegal. So he gave me two bottles of genuine Ballantine's scotch, which, if imbibed sparingly, he hoped would last through my freshman year and save me from the poisonous rotgut of some queazy Palo Alto bootlegger. Obviously, he knew *something* about the boozy habits of undergraduates but not enough. Those two precious bottles of Scotch were consumed in two nights, and I became addicted to the deliciously rich, creamy, and well-spiked beer available at speakeasies near the Stanford campus.

There were also nearby race tracks—Tanforan and Bay Meadows for flat racing in the daytime, the Bay Meadows dog track for gambling after dark. Since parimutuel betting had not yet been legalized, betting on all races was accomplished by the "option" system. All races were "claiming" races and the bettor's two-dollar ticket was an option to claim the horse after the race. The more options you purchased, the larger your claim, and if your horse won, placed, or came in third, your option ticket increased in value. Very few tickets were used for their stated purpose—to buy race horses or dogs. The tickets were cashed in or thrown away. I spent a lot of time with other disreputable undergraduates trying to get rich at the tracks. And when the tracks closed down, I banked an all-night roulette game in my dorm room, taking advantage of the house edge (0 and double 0) to turn a safe profit.

In short, I was having a good time and learning nothing about the digestive systems of frogs or the meaning of Plato's caves. I knew that if I were to remain at Stanford for four years, I might make the grade and get a diploma, but I would emerge unscathed by education. During my sophomore Christmas vacation, I pleaded with my dad to let me quit school and begin my full-time studio career. But my father had never gone to college, and he was determined that I should get the degree ~~that~~ he never had. So, with the help of one of the few college-educated Hollywood producers—Walter Wanger, Dartmouth '15—I was accepted for transfer to Dartmouth for my junior and senior years. In some respects that transfer could be regarded as jumping out of the frying pan into the fire because Dartmouth, isolated by two hundred and fifty miles from New York City and one hundred and thirty-five miles from Boston, was a noted breeding ground of alcoholism.

I transferred to Dartmouth in the fall of 1933, a time when the nation as a whole was becoming acutely aware of economic depression. Franklin D. Roosevelt had just moved into the White House, had declared a frightening but ostensibly necessary bank holiday, but had not yet been able to fulfill his promise to repeal the onerous Volstead Act which had resulted in what we called "Prohibition." (Beer was legalized at once but the repeal of the Volstead Act required the approval of states' legislatures. This wasn't achieved until December.)

Under these restrictive conditions, I had to find a reliable bootlegger at Dartmouth and did so across the river on the outskirts of Norwich, Vermont. His name was Joe Pilver. He had good contacts with Canadian suppliers and the Canadian border was less than two hundred miles away. He also sold straight alcohol by the gallon, and one could make two gallons of passable vodka by adding equal amounts of distilled water and the peel of two lemons. He also manufactured an odious-tasting applejack from the abundance of local apple cider, which he sold by the pint. But his principal claim to reliability—of which his customers were well aware—was that he supplied the alcoholic needs of the college president.

When beer was legalized, the college actually opened a tap room, serving inebriating quantities of 3.2 draft beer and pretzels, and it proved to be a successful effort to keep alcohol-loving students from hitting the treacherous mid-winter roads to nearby towns where beer would be easily obtained. There was a lot of barfing on the campus green, but fewer automobile accidents than if the school's community had remained totally "dry." (A popular poem on the Dartmouth campus went: "Old President Hopkins knew no peer. He gave us Doc Bowler and 3.2 beer.")

I'm not sure what these flirtations with alcohol have to do with "growing up with the movies," but they did prepare me for the seamy side of life at the studio and made me eager to attend the studio Christmas parties where secretaries and starlets, feigning "high's," if not actually under the influence, threw themselves at their bosses and at an occasional youthful interloper like me. Experiences like that and the one with the film crew in Panama were, I suppose, intended to prepare me for my "destiny" as a big shot at the studio, a destiny that was never fulfilled. But they made for an interesting adolescence and provided me with movie-oriented yarns that would hold the interest of latter-day film students.

Needless to say, moviegoing was always an important part of my youth. Today we are well aware of the MPAA ratings system and we know that PG means "parental guidance suggested," so that no one under a given age can attend without an adult. But in my early days in New York City I would stand on a Broadway sidewalk twenty or thirty yards from the Bunny Theater (named for a well-known comedian, not the rabbit) and stop a man who was obviously heading for the box-office with a dime in my hand and a plea: "Take me into the movies, mister?" As I recall, you had to be twelve years old in those days to get into *any* movie without an adult.

As I got older, growing up in the Hollywood area, I was able to go to the movies on passes. The Warner Theaters pass was a medallion, good in perpetuity to admit two. The Fox West Coast pass was a card to be renewed every year, and Fox West Coast theaters were very common in Southern California, featuring Fox and MGM pictures. My friend Schulberg had a pass that was good for the downtown Paramount, though most of the Paramount-Publix chain was in the Midwest and East.

I invented some lame excuse to con my parents into okaying a transfer from John Burroughs, a public junior high in our neighborhood, to the private L. A. Coaching School—a splendid institution with intimate, intense classes, to be sure, but the principal attraction for me was that each day's classes ended at 12:30 P.M. Since the Coaching School was close to downtown, this meant that my cronies and I could finish classes, have a bite to eat at the corner drugstore (drugstores had soda fountains in those days, where they served hot roast beef sandwiches with mashed potatoes and gravy, milk shakes, and delicious desserts), and head downtown to the Metropolitan and the Paramount to see two movies in a single afternoon. (My cronies included a talented musician, Leon Becker, who later abandoned a career as a concert pianist to become a movie production genius, and my friend Budd Schulberg.)

Actually, there was a certain competition and rivalry in this moviegoing. Schulberg's father was then head of production at Paramount, my father a major figure at MGM, and the Metropolitan and Paramount the flagships for exhibiting the product of each studio. Naturally, we were in disagreement as to the relative merits of *Now We're In the Air* (a Paramount comedy about the Air Force, with the comedy team of Wallace Beery and Raymond Hatton) and *Rookies* (MGM's comedy about the army with Karl Dane and George K. Arthur) and these arguments could only be settled by the box-office figures listed in the weekly *Variety.*

Readers who remember the old movie palaces will recall that there was once a stage show to go with a first-run feature movie. The Metropolitan, a Fox-West Coast theater, featured a show put together by Fanchon and Marco, with Fanchon's brother Rube Wolf conducting the onstage band and introducing the vaudeville acts. The Paramount show was presided over by a succession of emcees, including Eddie Peabody (who played a solo banjo and led the band) and Gene Morgan, a comedian who always wore a too-small green fedora to let you know he was Irish and who ended up playing comedy roles in movies.

First-run theaters sometimes linked their stage shows to the content of feature movies if a long run was expected. The Carthay Circle Theater, off Wilshire Boulevard and far from downtown Los Angeles, was an example of this. I recall that when they ran a silent World War I film with Colleen Moore and Gary Cooper called *Lilac Time*, there was a stage show featuring a couple of singers expressing their passion beside the hull of a crashed World War I fighter plane. I also recall seeing a George Arliss movie called *The Green Goddess* at the Capitol Theater in New York when I was about six years old, in which a lot of steam came out of the orchestra pit, followed by a bevy of green devils, the sight of which caused me to have nightmares for months thereafter.

On the other hand, New York's Radio City Music Hall, the premier movie showcase in the United States, had elaborate hour-long stage shows that celebrated the seasons rather than the movie currently being shown. People often reserved seats for the celebrated Christmas show a year in advance, not caring a whit whether the Music Hall would be running an Astaire-Rogers musical or *Random*

Harvest. This was true of the Easter and Fourth of July shows as well, all of which would feature the famed high-kicking Rockettes.

I became so addicted to "free" movies that when I enrolled at Dartmouth I went to see Art Barwood, manager of the Hanover movie theater, to ask for a pass, even though, as I recall, admission was only twenty-five cents. Barwood asked why and I told him, with what must have seemed like considerable arrogance, that my father was an important producer and I never paid to see movies. He said, "Well, you're going to pay here unless the Boston office of MGM confirms your story."

The Boston office *did* confirm my story and I got a pass, even though, as a movie reviewer for the college newspaper, I could have got in for nothing anyway. But to this day I find it difficult to pay to see a movie. My father died in 1949 and there were no passes forthcoming after that except for passes to my uncle's theaters in the New York area. My uncle, an exhibitor, got wealthy partly with theater ownership but more so because of his pioneering introduction of food and drink sales in movie theaters. On his periodic visits to the West Coast—to see his mother, who lived with us—he would get into heated arguments, claiming that he, an exhibitor, knew more about movie audiences than my father or his producer friends.

Like so many movie moguls, my father always had projection facilities at home, and projectionists came to our house at the studio's expense to run rushes of movies that were in production or new movies from MGM or other studios. Whenever my parents had company, a new movie would be run after dinner. Nowadays, we have many sources bringing new and old movies directly to the TV sets in our homes, and when there is nothing interesting being broadcast, we can always go to our local video rental stores and, for a nominal sum, bring home to our VCRs some juicy tidbit we may have missed.

Being the son of a Hollywood bigshot had its rewards and its drawbacks. I dreaded being seen in the family limousine. When the chauffeur had to drive me to school on a rainy day, for example, I would insist that he drop me off a block from L. A. High so that none of my classmates could see me in the proverbial lap of luxury. And I can remember going to a premiere at Grauman's Chinese Theater with thousands of people lining the streets through which our limousine would creep. And a group of girls peered in through the windows of the car, looked straight at little me in my tuxedo, and said, "Oh, it's nobody."

On the other hand, when I traveled with my parents, I enjoyed the advantages of the privileged class. When we went to Europe in 1925, we were in first class on the *Berengaria* and our dinner companion was the British High Commissioner for Palestine, Sir Herbert Samuel. When we went to Nice, we met film director Rex Ingram and his gorgeous wife, Alice Terry. In Berlin, we visited UFA and met director E. A. Dupont and his stars in *Variety*, Lya de Putti and Emil Jannings. Fritz Lang was not yet shooting *Metropolis*, but some of the massive sets had already been built.

One trouble with celebrity when it brushes off on the very young is that people forget that you are indeed "very young." And, in this connection, I can recall being taken on exotic location trips with film crews, being sent to bed early, but being very much aware of the enticing but forbidden hanky-panky going on in adjoining hotel rooms. This exposure to the sexual shenanigans of my father and his associates may have had something to do with my reluctance to associate with "girls" until my senior year in high school. All my birthday parties were strictly stag affairs. Many were held in my father's backyard projection room where, after a preview of some new movie, we would take off our jackets and ties, and choose up sides, with half of those present dedicated to giving me—the birthday boy—a solid swat for each year of my life, while the defenders would try to protect me. We enjoyed these fights even if we sometimes wrecked some furniture. The only trouble was that, as time passed, we grew a little too big for these antics. The stag parties were discontinued on what I think was my fifteenth birthday when one guest was taken off in an ambulance, with a crushed disk in his back.

At a later birthday party at a Santa Monica beach club—this one included girls—we were entertained by Ted Healy and the Three Stooges, courtesy of my father who was making a series of shorts with them at that time. Even as late as the forties, my father presented my children with a Chistmas recording (which I still have) introduced by Jimmy Durante, who says, "Joannie and Gerry, this is Jimmy Durante. I want to introduce you to someone you know and who loves you very much—your grandfather."

So the plusses of having a big-shot father far outweighed the minusses, and one of the big plusses was going away for weekends with my parents to various California vacation areas. This penchant by Angelenos to "get away" led to the construction of the finest vacation resort of all—the hotel and facilities at Agua Caliente in Baja, California, a province of Mexico and no more than forty-five minutes' drive from San Diego or Coronado. It was built in the early thirties by a consortium headed by a noted local sportsman and gambler, Baron Long, and with ex-heavyweight champion Jack Dempsey, then married to actress Estelle Taylor, as his window-dressing partner.

Caliente was intended to offer high-flying U.S. citizens a taste of what they might find at Monte Carlo—and then some. There was a magnificent casino, a splendid flat racing track for thoroughbreds in the afternoons (where the noted Australian horse, Phar Lap, established his American reputation) and dog racing at night. Agua Caliente means "hot water" and the place was indeed a spa, but there was also a splendid golf course, tennis courts, two or three restaurants featuring specific cuisines, including Mexican, and a night club.

Needless to say, Caliente became a major attraction for the Hollywood crowd from the day it opened. My singular memory of the place goes back to the New Year's weekend of 1934. I was twenty, a junior at Dartmouth, and on vacation to the West Coast for the Christmas break. The January 2 Rose Bowl game in Pasadena was to pit Stanford, champion of the Pacific Coast Conference, against lowly Columbia, which had somehow managed to finish its Eastern schedule without a defeat. (This was before the days of the contract between the PCC and the Big Ten.)

Having spent two years at Stanford before transferring to Dartmouth, I was determined to get to Pasadena to see that game. So was a New York visitor—Howard Dietz, a noted lyricist (*Dancing in the Dark*), head of national publicity for MGM and a Columbia alumnus.

Dietz arranged to have a chauffeur-driven limousine pick us up at the Caliente hotel at 7 A.M. on January 2. Rain was coming down in sheets and we were about halfway to Pasadena when the Cadillac ran through a deep puddle and stalled. The chauffeur couldn't get it started. Dietz, by this time several sheets to the wind from swigs of cognac, told me to get out of the car; we'd hitch our way to Pasadena and if the Cadillac could be repaired, the driver would catch up with us. Three or four rides later, we were passed by the limo, asked our driver to honk and we resumed our luxurious transport. We reached the game on time, but it was still raining and the field was a quagmire.

Stanford, coached at the time by Tiny Thornhill and with an all-American back named Bobby Grayson, was famous for its versatile running attack and was an overwhelming favorite over lowly Columbia. which had a good first team but no depth. The soggy field and Columbia's sturdy defense kept the powerful Stanford offense at bay and a versatile Columbia back, Al Barabas, pulled a fake reverse and scored for Lou Little's Lions in the second quarter. From then on, it was all Stanford, but they never scored. It was one of the biggest upsets in Rose Bowl history: Columbia 7, Stanford 0.

Dietz, who had finished a fifth of cognac with a little help from me, was ecstatic. We were in a front row box. He realized that he was one of the few Columbia rooters in the stands. "Let's tear down the goalposts," he said. And we went onto the muddy field and tried, though without success. When we got to the parking area—which was at that time a neighboring golf course—and couldn't find the chauffeur or the limo, Dietz didn't care. His team had won. He was whooping it up. We hitched a ride back to Los Angeles.

I had gone to college (Stanford) in the fall of 1931 and took great pride in my father's achievements at that time. Although he took no screen credit, his film *The Champ* won Academy awards for writer Frances Marion and for actor Wallace Beery in the spring of 1932. That same year Helen Hayes was named best actress for her work in another of his films, *The Sin of Madelon Claudet.* The following year, Marie Dressler won best actress for her work in his film *Min and Bill.* All of his pictures (including *Possessed, Emma, Tugboat Annie, Christopher Bean,* and *New Morals for Old*) had class and clout. Marie Dressler, who worked almost exclusively for him, was judged to be the most popular female actress in America. Then came my father's heart attack.

It was 1933, at the height of his success in the business, and he was forced to take a year off to recuperate. (Irving Thalberg had a heart attack a few months later and also had to take a year off.) When my father went back to work, things were never the same. With my father and Thalberg gone, producers at MGM began to put their names on films. Rivalries for stars and directors were rife. Nicholas Schenck of the New York office sent some of his henchmen to the West Coast to keep an eye on what was happening and to throw their weight around wherever needed—which proved to be, for the most part, wherever they chose.

When I came home for Christmas vacation during my senior year at college (1934), I was appalled by my father's loss of standing at the studio. I actually wrote a lousy one-act play that mirrored his situation as an executive on the skids, with those around him contributing to his loss of confidence. It was called *Defeated* and although I entered it (without success) in a student playwriting contest at Dartmouth, my real purpose in writing it was to express my feelings to my father. Looking back, I realize it was a rather cruel thing to do. Here is a quote from that play—spoken by the producer's son to his despondent father:

> MILTON: I know what it is, Dad. I'm sure I do. It's these guys around this studio. These Greenbaums and Markhams. These wise guys have got you scared. You've made a couple of pictures that didn't go well, and they've tried darn hard to make sure you knew it. . . . Now you're in a spot where you're afraid to make any decisions, for fear of being wrong. I know what you are thinking. Too old! I'm through! I just don't get ideas any more. . . . These are young, active. I'm old. I've had my heyday. That's a lot of rubbish. You just know about twice as much as any of them.

New producers had been hired. Within a few years, the total number of producers on the lot—which had been two or three in the twenties—would rise to over twenty. My father was undoubtedly the oldest. He was, after all, one of the founders of the company, and as such he expected a certain amount of respect. What he got instead was condescension and even derision from the newcomers. His job was secure enough, but his wings had been clipped and he no longer had the power that came with the backing of Mayer and Thalberg. My friend Budd's father, B. P. Schulberg, used to tell me that without my father's movies, MGM never would have survived the twenties. But Schulberg himself was to lose his own position as the head of Paramount at about the same time that my father's prestige began to fall, and before the end of the decade he had to run a full page ad in a Hollywood trade paper, seeking a job. He got it.

My father was never very happy at MGM when he returned after recuperating from his heart attack, and he ultimately began to consider offers for other affiliations. Somehow, he never had the nerve to leave. Part of that was due to the advice of his very conservative mother, who always had a decisive influence on his life. "You'd be a fool to leave," she would say. "Always remember that L. B. (meaning Mayer) is your bread and butter." But once you accept the fact that someone in authority is your "bread and butter," you can ultimately be forced to eat shit. And that, in some ways, is precisely what happened to my father in the early forties.

None of the films Harry Rapf made after 1938 was really very good and two of them, *Ice Follies of 1939* and *Forty Little Mothers* (with Eddie Cantor) were really clinkers. Then someone had a bright idea. Why not set up a new unit to encourage new talent? Dore Schary, an ambitious young Turk who had had some success as a writer, takes credit for the idea and was indeed promoted from writer to producer when the unit was launched. But there was a catch imposed by the MGM brass: Schary would share control of the new experimental unit with a man of long experience, Harry Rapf.

According to Schary (in his self-serving autobiography, *Heyday*), he (Schary) was to have complete creative control of the unit's output. Harry Rapf would be no more than a figure-head with control over budgets and no more. (The unit was, however, called the "Rapf-Schary unit.") When Rapf stepped over the line with less than flattering comments about the work of some of the young directors (again according to Schary's autobiography), Schary blew his stack, complained to the top brass and brought about a dismal confrontation between Louis B. Mayer and my father, in which "bread and butter" Mayer took the side of the up-and-coming Schary and told my father to pack his things and leave the studio.

My father's confrontation with Mayer really did take place, but for quite different reasons and with quite a different result, as told to me by Sam Marx, one of the producers in the Rapf-Schary unit, who has written at length about MGM history. In the first place, the notion that Schary was to have complete creative control of the unit was a Schary fabrication. There were seven or eight associate producers assigned to the unit. Three of them—Sam Marx, Arthur Field, and Irving Starr, were to work under Rapf; four—William Wright, Bernie Ziedman, Bernie Fineman, and Jack Chertok—would work under Schary. The unit turned out some unusual low-budget films that got good reviews and did well at the box office, beginning with *Joe Smith, American* and followed by *Journey for Margaret, Lassie Come Home, Bataan,* and many others. My father took pride not only in the pictures made by producers under his supervision (the *Lassie* films, *Bataan,* and *Affairs of Martha*) but also in the Schary films (*Joe Smith, Journey for Margaret,* and *Pilot #5*). As far as I could see at the time, there was no rivalry. I was wrong. The ambitious Schary didn't like the idea of sharing credit with the older man. He created an incident and, for a day or two, he prevailed—he got my father fired. Then, according to his account, he regretted his action and asked L. B. Mayer to back down on his edict and to reinstate my father with the clear understanding that he was not to interfere in the future with the production process.

What really happened—and there is written evidence of this—is that all but one of the associate producers in the unit signed a letter to

Mayer supporting my father's creative role in production and asking for his reinstatement. My father was aware of this action, thanked his staff, and was restored to his position. Shortly thereafter, Schary, possibly still chafing at the idea of sharing credit, asked to leave the unit to produce major features on his own. He subsequently worked on two projects which were never made, and he left the studio. One Schary project was an allegorical western ~~that was~~ intended to reflect the rise of fascism for which he hired Sinclair Lewis to do the screenplay. The other was intended to be an offbeat history of movies—about a midwestern theater owner who had been greeting Hollywood celebrities as they passed through his town (a place like Dodge City, Kansas) on the Super Chief. I knew about the latter because I gave Schary my collection of MGM yearbooks from the twenties—and never got it back.

The experimental film unit that had been known as "Rapf-Schary" continued for another year and a half under my father's sole supervision. The best movies made during this period were *Our Vines Have Tender Grapes* and *The Canterville Ghost.* Then the producers and directors, having proven their ability, were given a chance to work outside the unit and my father was kicked upstairs to the executive committee, which decided matters of story policy for the entire company.

Schary had left the studio. My father, part of the executive committee, could hire writers to work on scripts and could produce movies if his scripts were approved. (*The Adventures of Gallant Bess* was the best film he made during this period.) He was still drawing a four-figure salary, about a third of what he once earned, though with a smaller office and no power. He didn't leave when he was riding high; he couldn't leave now, because no one wanted him.

I told him to retire. He said he couldn't. He was carrying a big load of life insurance that required payment of thousands of dollars a month to finance trusts that would be set up, at his death, for my brother and me. I urged him to take the cash value of those policies and to relieve himself of paying premiums, but he refused. That insurance turned out to be the bulk of his estate. He owned no shares in Loews Incorporated, having taken cash when the founders were offered a share of the company in 1930 and, with the stock market crash fresh in mind, his mother had told him to take the money and run. It proved to be a mistake, and now ~~that he was~~ in his mid-sixties he was paying for it.

He died very suddenly of a heart attack on February 6, 1949. The last sixteen years of his life had been, after all, lived on borrowed time. Doctors had told him when he had the heart attack in 1932 that he didn't have long to live. I wish ~~that~~ the last years of his life could have been more satisfying. I caused him considerable pain by being black-listed, as I shall explain later. And my brother Matthew had not yet begun the illustrious career he was to have in television as the executive producer of such shows as *Ben Casey* and *Kojak*. My father would have been very proud of him, maybe even pleased by the fact that I, the wayward son, ended up as a college professor, adding academic respectability to what we considered the family business. I'm not sure, but I like to think that somehow, somewhere, he knows.

Chapter 3

The Studio (MGM)

The MGM studio was my father's workplace until he died. He went to the studio every morning the way other men went to their offices or shops. He would drive through the front gate on Washington Boulevard in the morning and pull over to the curb adjacent to the walkway between the administration building and the wardrobe building which was fronted by a lawn with a prodigious fig tree. Someone—I don't know who—would drive his car to a parking place on the lot.

He would then climb the outside metal staircase to the second-floor balcony that led to his office and to Irving Thalberg's, which adjoined it. There was easy access between the offices and their respective secretaries shared another space down a short hallway, next to which was a waiting room. Persons who wanted to see Thalberg and could get by the factotum who guarded the entrance downstairs had a long wait. Thalberg, a night worker, arrived late, always in his limousine, which was driven by a versatile black man known as Slickem.

Slickem, after dropping his boss at the executive building, parked the car somewhere and took over as proprietor of the studio's shoe-shine stand. He also did bit parts from time to time. (Oscar, the boot-black at Schulberg's Paramount studio, performed similar functions there and his memory is preserved by cameo appearances in *Sullivan's Travels* and *Sunset Boulevard*.)

The MGM lot, as I said earlier, was my father's workplace. It was also my playground. Every Saturday during the school year (they worked a six-day week in those days, before the industry was unionized), I went with my father to the studio and often with a crony who was usually Budd Schulberg, because he and I knew best how to act

39

out our own versions of fantastic stories based on movies then in production or recently completed on sets and with whatever props were
available. We could do much better than the usual childhood "cops
and robbers" and "cowboys and Indians." MGM had inherited the
uncompleted production of *Ben Hur.* There were chariots, sections of
galley ships, and old Roman and Jerusalem street sets, and the prop
department had Roman shields, helmets, and swords.

Our usual procedure, after my father dropped us at the front gate
near his office, was to go to the prop department and outfit ourselves
with suitable equipment for the story we intended to act out on the
back lot sets. In *Ben Hur* days, it would be helmets, shields, and
swords. A year later, when a movie about World War I, *The Big Parade,* was the studio's major production, we outfitted ouselves as Yan-
kee doughboys with unloaded rifles, doughboy helmets, bayonets,
and all.

The prop department (whose manager was the ubiquitous Edwin
Willis, credited on many MGM films for set decoration) was a place
of pure magic for imaginative youngsters like us. It was a square brick
building three or four stories tall that looked like a warehouse, but on
each of its floors were exotic accoutrements from scores of movies
with which we could recreate all periods of history and every part of
the world. One of the most interesting and workable sections was that
of "Western" props, which included poker tables and captain's chairs,
roulette wheels, moose heads, mahogany bars, and a priceless collection of ancient slot machines and music boxes—all in working order.

On the back lot itself there were several tanks that were meant to
simulate ponds or lakes or even the sea. There were small boats and
in one pond were a number of artificial ice floes, which floated nicely
but were quite unsteady. It was not unusual for me or one of my
friends to fall into a tank from time to time, after which we would
have to go to the wardrobe department which, with the usual studio
nepotism, was run by my uncle Joe Rapf. There, we asked for some
dry clothes, which, when they were provided in the proper size, sometimes made us look like characters in a Dickens novel.

Budd Schulberg's father was head of Paramount and my father was
one of the heads of MGM. We chased down autographs on both lots
but preferred MGM as a playground because it had more space than
Paramount and more glamorous sets to act out our stories.

Nevertheless, there was an intense rivalry between Budd and me as
to the merits of our fathers' movies and as to the box-office results of

Paramount versus Metro-Goldwyn-Mayer films. One manifestation of this in 1929 and 1930 was a competition between us as to which songs from our fathers' movies were played most frequently on the radio.

Musicals were popular fare when sound was introduced, and all the major studios imported singers, dancers, and songwriters. Paramount had Maurice Chevalier and the songs of Ralph Rainger and Leo Robin. MGM had Charlie King and the songs of Nacio Herb Brown and Arthur Freed. For a while it was "Beyond the Blue Horizon" (Chevalier) versus "Wedding of the Painted Doll" (King). Later it was Chevalier's "Mimi" versus Ramon Novarro's "The Pagan Love Song." What we did—on the honor system—was to keep track of how many times these tunes were played on our respective radios. Today, of course, publications such as *Variety* and *Billboard* will give a radio or juke box count on every popular number. In fact, when Lucky Strike inaugurated its popular radio program *The Hit Parade* within a year or two of our competition, they would list songs, including those from movies, in order of popularity. We no longer had to continue our honor system competition.

Suffice it to say that the MGM studio was a self-contained film factory—from idea to finished product. I have already mentioned two of its departments—props and wardrobe—but there were many more.

Casting headquarters was on Washington Boulevard, near what was called "the front gate," which, I am told, still stands despite the renovations of the Sony company which acquired the property in 1990. (MGM had actually been sold to William Fox in 1929 but the deal was subsequently cancelled.) There was a reason for casting being on the main drag, for it was through these doors that the call for extras would be filled. There were sometimes long lines of day players—either wearing their own modern wardrobes or yet to be costumed—waiting, like longshoreman at a shake-up, to see whether they would be chosen for the jobs that, in the twenties, paid five dollars a day for members of the crowd, ten dollars for smaller groups, and twenty-five dollars if there were any chance of being seen in a close-up. Higher rates always prevailed for "dress extras" and those who spoke lines.

The editing rooms were, by design, also near the front gates as were the front offices that housed the producers. (There was a bridge to connect the executive offices to the editing rooms.) Many of the editing rooms were on the second floor of a long building above the projection rooms. Because of the metal balcony that ran the length of the building and the various doorways that led onto it, the location could be filmed as an army headquarters or even—with the doors replaced by bars—as a prison.

The camera department had its own building. The head man was John Arnold, an ex-cinematographer himself, and there were at least twenty-five cameramen on the payroll on a year-round basis. They were busy most of the time, since the studio turned out between forty and fifty features a year, plus a number of short subjects.

Many of the top female stars had their pet cinematographers, as each woman was convinced that only one man could handle whatever blemishes—and there were few—that she had. Bill Daniels shot all of Norma Shearer's films and Ollie Marsh was the sine qua non for Garbo and Joan Crawford. One actress, Jean Harlow, actually married her pet cinematographer, Hal Rossen.

There was also a bevy of skilled portrait photographers and with this art form as well, the stars and studio brass had their favorites, some of whom have been immortalized in coffee-table books that are still available. Probably the most famous was George Hurrell, who came to MGM briefly in the early thirties because he could "shoot" Norma Shearer without revealing that one of her eyes was slightly askew. My father used Clarence Sinclair Bull to shoot his portraits as well as some pictures of our family.

The studio had special departments for construction and painting, a plaster shop, and a film processing laboratory (where I once worked), outside of which was a lofty brick smokestack where unwanted negatives were burned every morning. There was the always fascinating special effects department, which handled the construction of miniatures—used to simulate ships, trains, burning buildings, and even desert caravans. There was one entire production stage devoted to "process shots," where actors were photographed against rear-projection screens, usually to simulate situations against moving backgrounds such as the rear window of a car or the side window of a train, or, when the actor or actress was placed on an electric horse, the passing countryside.

There was a police department, a commissary, a barber shop, transportation and an ongoing school so that child actors could satisfy the legal requirements for education by doing daily lessons.

Then there were departments associated with the preparation of story material—the story departments and research. The story department at MGM actually had two primary functions—to seek out and deal with writers and to do the same with story material. I think that the script department, headed by a woman named Edith Farrell for as long as I can remember, also fell under the aegis of the story department. The script department consisted of fifty or sixty skilled stenographers who worked individually with the more important writers and comprised a pool to be drawn upon by those less highly placed.

In teaching film classes I have always stressed that the history of movies has from its inception been profoundly affected by the search for story material. To accept this, you have to believe that movies are—with exceptions that should be obvious—a story-telling medium. Let me describe the work of story departments.

MGM, for example, employed about sixty readers in the mid-thirties. It was their job to comb through every conceivable literary source for possible movie material and to synopsize that material so that producers could tell at a glance or with a short reading whether the subject was of interest to them.

There was tremendous competition among producers for acquisition of literary properties. The very idea of genre was certainly nurtured, if not born, in the synopses that readers prepared for producers. A single word after "Type," on page one of a synopsis would be Western, Gangster, Adventure, Romance, Family, Spy, Detective, Historical, Biographical, and so forth.

As for classics, which might be in the public domain, they, too, were synopsized on request. And if a producer showed some interest in *Silas Marner*, for example, he could hire a junior writer at a low salary to work for six weeks and that would establish his claim to that subject for two years, after which he could renew his claim with six additional weeks' work by a low-paid writer. (David Selznick made two Dickens novels—*David Copperfield* and *A Tale of Two Cities*—into films, but it was said that he had tied up all of Dickens' works; when Fox expressed interest in making a new version of *Oliver Twist*, they had to negotiate the rights with Selznick.) Preposterous as this arrangement might seem, it did provide employment for many junior writers, which was an apprentice classification that could only exist under the old studio system, and many of us were grateful for it.

We were also grateful for the research department, which functioned very much the way libraries do, with experts capable of digging up what the writers needed to know about any given period or place and then what the set designers and costume people needed. Writers, young or old, inevitably took advantage of this department during the first week or weeks of an assignment while waiting for the ideas to come. Another ploy that postponed turning in the first pages was asking to see a few movies that had some bearing on your current subject—whether made by MGM or others. Studios serviced each other in this regard.

I haven't mentioned the publicity department because I was never quite certain how it worked. The "publicity" part was clear enough. One representative of the department was assigned to each feature that was being produced. It was his or her job to see that sufficient stills were taken for publicity purposes (the still cameramen on the set and the portrait photographers were part of the publicity department), that information about the course of production was fed to the press, and that interviews were arranged with the featured players and with the director. But there was another side to the workings of the publicity department that made it a bit like the CIA. It had the task of preventing *bad* publicity about any production or anyone connected with the studio. And this could lead to some pretty fancy footwork with the press, with the D.A.'s office and, sometimes, with the police—as happened with the controversial suicide of producer Paul Bern and, later, the death of his widow, the glamorous sexpot, Jean Harlow.

Although some of what I have described pertains particularly to studios during the silent era, much of it carried over into studio operation after the introduction of sound. In this regard, it is important to note that sound changed the studios noticeably—in terms of their physical plants, in the way they operated, and in terms of control.

The nature of movies and their management has always been affected by technical innovation—even though the basic principle of the camera's mechanism has not changed appreciably since it was invented in the last century. As film historians know, Edison even demonstrated synchronous sound with film at the end of the nineteenth century. (His short filmed commercials for Dewar's whiskey are still available.)

I remember going with my father into a Gaumont projection room in Paris in 1925 and seeing a demonstration of sound films. Like many of his colleagues who "turned down the Vitaphone," my father was not impressed. (He also saw his first demonstration of neon lights on that trip; he could have invested in the American rights, but didn't see the advantage over the old bulb series of lighting!)

Film historians report that the heads of all the major studios turned down the opportunity to introduce sound. Silent films were a very profitable venture. Why change? (George S. Kauffman and Moss Hart wrote a hit play *Once in a Lifetime* in which their producer, Herman Glogauer (modelled on Adolph Zukor of Paramount) is known as "the man who turned down the Vitaphone.") Most studios did, however, experiment with technical innovations because movie attendance was being adversely affected by the growing popularity of radio in the twenties, as it would be by TV in the fifties. Radio kept people out of movie theaters, and it also made them sound-oriented. After all, 40 percent of U.S. homes had radios in 1927. Color was one innovation that producers were willing to try, using Technicolor's two-color process, which lacked reds but was subdued enough to be pleasing to the eye. The process was also expensive, so after the first color feature, *Toll of the Sea,* with the Asian star Anna Mae Wong, in 1922, color was limited to single sequences, as in the 1925 *Phantom of the Opera.* Douglas Fairbanks, *The Black Pirate,* made in 1926, was the first all-color feature.

Old Ironsides, a historical movie that was made in 1927 about the U.S. move on Tripoli, used a big screen for the first time in metropolitan movie houses. I saw the premiere of *Old Ironsides* (much of which was shot at the isthmus on nearby Catalina Island) because it was produced by Budd Schulberg's dad for Paramount. I remember that the movie was seen on a normal-sized screen until about five minutes before the climax, when *Old Ironsides* was about to sail into battle off the shores of Tripoli. The stage curtains were pulled back and the projected picture of the majestic sailing ship grew to three times its normal size. The first night audience applauded.

But sound, as it was introduced by Warner Bros. with the Vitaphone system and by Fox with Movietone, proved to be the big bonanza, and by 1929 when all the major studios had converted, 100 million people a week were paying their way into movie theaters.

My father had a separate building in our backyard which served as a projection room. Within a year after the sensational reception of *The Jazz Singer,* our projection machines were converted to handle the disc system known as Vitaphone—not very complicated, really. To install sound, one had only to add a sixteen-inch turntable with an umbilical cord or cable so that it could be driven by the projector. And, of course, the necessary amplifiers and speakers. The sound was on a record that played at $33\frac{1}{3}$ revolutions per minute (the speed of the later consumer LPs) but the needle was placed at the center and worked its way out.

The Fox Movietone system, which proved in the long run to be more practical, provided the source of sound on the film itself—a narrow strip along one edge of the 35-millimeter stock with optical striations to activate a photoelectric cell that sent the same impulses to the amplifiers and speaker systems that could be produced through the grooves of a record. The sound was originally recorded on a separate strip of film and edited alongside the picture by using a sprocketed device, called a "synchronizer," which kept film and sound in perfect "sync." Both sound and picture could subsequently be printed on a single strand and shipped in this fashion to the theaters where, because sound and picture were wedded, a movie would not get out of sync, as it sometimes did with Vitaphone when a needle skipped a groove on the disk.

There was one big disadvantage to this system, however: Old theater projectors had to be scrapped and new ones purchased, and so the battle of the systems lasted about two years. Most big theaters were equipped with both systems, and studios released their films in both. It was an expensive procedure, involving the soundproofing of interior theater walls, but the theaters converted quickly—even though as late as 1931 there were five or six thousand theaters in the United States which ran only silent films and a few small Hollywood studios which produced nothing else.

Needless to say, with the novelty and instant popularity of sound, the move toward the use of color was temporarily stalled. Technicolor, the company that had pioneered the process under the direction of Herbert and Nathalie Kalmus, continued to improve its technique, moving from a two-color to a three-color process in 1932. And Walt Disney (who had the foresight to adopt sound for all of his shorts, beginning with *Steamboat Willie* in 1927) worked exclusively in the three-color process beginning in 1933 with *Flowers and Trees.* But the only major three-color process feature in the early thirties was the unsuccessful *Becky Sharp* in 1935. *Nothing Sacred* was produced using this process in 1937, and *Gone with the Wind* and some sequences of *The Wizard of Oz* were filmed in 1939.

My father tried to introduce a rival color system at MGM in 1947 when he made a horse movie called *The Adventures of Gallant Bess.* The process was Cinecolor and it differed from Technicolor in that it had colored emulsion on both sides of the film stock. I became familiar with Cinecolor because that company gave my father a dozen or more Ub Iwerks cartoons which had been made with the process in the thirties and I had eager young children who remember them to this day. (Some of the subjects that are still available on videotape are *The Sunshine Makers, The King's Tailor, The Pincushion Man, Jack Frost*, and *Brom, the Headless Horseman*).

More than the advent of color in film, it was the conversion to sound that caused the most significant changes in studio facilities and operations. The first things that had to go were the "shooting stages," flimsy hangar-like buildings with thin walls, many having glass roofs to let in shreds of daylight. They were large and could house the sets for several productions at the same time. Indeed, it was not unusual to see two or three movies being shot on the same stage. The shooting stages had to be replaced, at first on the same sites, by sound stages—large structures with thick, padded walls and double sound-proofed doors. High up on one wall of these structures were projecting booths with a full view of the floor below (much like a guard's lookout point in a prison yard). Here sat the recording engineer, with connections to the mikes on the floor below and to the sound department where the sound was actually recorded on film and on disk. (The reason for recording studio work on a disk was so that it could be played back immediately for review. The sound that was recorded on film had to be processed in a lab, along with the picture, and would not be available until the following day.)

There were social changes as well as physical ones. The informality on the set seemed to disappear. For one thing, utter silence was required during every take. For another, location shooting—except for silent sequences—became almost impossible. Exteriors of houses, jungle settings, and gardens were recreated indoors. There would be too much extraneous noise if they tried to shoot on location or on the back lot—my old playground. They even built a simulation of Canada's Chilkoot Pass indoors for a movie called *The Trail of '98*.

Sound also introduced new departments and new personnel to the studio. There was music, of course. The studio had always had a music department of sorts, because silent movies were sent out with sheet music as suggestions to local orchestras, organists, and piano players. Now studios acquired staff composers, arrangers, and the personnel for full studio orchestras. The studios' need for musicians was a bonanza for many of those who lost their jobs in the pits of first-run movie theaters. And some of the prestigious pit conductors—Hugo Riesenfeld, Erno Rapee, and Nathaniel Finston, to name a few—ended up doing scores for movies. One pit conductor, Leo Forbstein, who had led the orchestra at Grauman's Million Dollar (a first-run movie theater in downtown Los Angeles), ended up as the head of the music department at Warner Bros.

Singing and dancing were perfectly suited to the new sound medium, and the studios began their competition to lure the best songsmiths from Tin Pan Alley. This led to importing singers and dancers from the stage, hiring dance directors and voice coaches, and even to signing opera stars such as Lawrence Tibbett, Gladys Swarthout, Lily Pons, and Grace Moore.

In the meantime, sound led to another kind of importation, which not only changed the studios but the nature of the Hollywood community as well. Actors, directors, and writers were recruited from the Broadway stage. After all, if movies were to feature sound, they would require the skills of those who were accustomed to dealing with speech as well as image. Among actors, this made the English very desirable because of their clear-cut enunciation and the snob quality of a British accent. Among writers, the playwrights were sought because they could handle dialogue.

The new personnel from the East brought with them a social awareness that had not yet reached their California colleagues. The actors were union members in Actors' Equity, and the playwrights had won definitive authors' rights in the Dramatists Guild. Many had definite left wing leanings.

The talent hunt was on, and many stage and recording celebrities were brought to Hollywood. Some made the grade; others did not because they lacked that mysterious quality known as "screen presence." Among the failed celebrities were John McCormack, Sophie Tucker, Fanny Brice, and Texas Guinan. You tried 'em and if they didn't work, they went home.

Sound really changed the industry. It killed a lot of small studios, brought Warners from last to first place and established the importance of some new ones like Columbia, 20th Century–Fox, and RKO. But the most profound change of all in the industry was in the shift of financial control. The cost of converting studios and theaters to sound and the need to pay for the patent use of equipment owned by Bell Laboratories, RCA, and General Electric shifted financial control of the industry from movie moguls and their friends and relations to Wall Street. In the thirties, the movie industry was described as the fourth largest business in the country, but this was largely because of the vast real estate holdings involved in the exhibition end of the business. The government would put an end to this after the war, with its order under the anti-trust laws that production must be divorced from exhibition.

Movies and their production were also profoundly affected by changes in the social structure (though scholars can make a good case for the opposite: that movies have a powerful effect on society itself). The Depression era of the thirties provides a pretty good example of this interplay. Even if the studio family spirit of the twenties, which involved picnics, golf tournaments, and noontime shindigs, had continued, it would have been shaken up by the influx of new people from the East—writers, actors, directors, and musicians—many of whom were union members, some of whom were radicals, most of whom were more politically and socially aware than their Hollywood colleagues. They had a lot to do with changing the social climate in Hollywood. But so did events on the national scene—the move toward union recognition and, in the late thirties, a concern with the threat of fascism abroad.

Three events at MGM destroyed that studio's family spirit in the thirties and caused my father—who was part of management—to become alienated from many of the writers, actors, and directors who had worked for him and felt a loyalty to him. The first was management's attempt to introduce a 50 percent salary cut in 1931 and the subsequent discovery that the company executives gave themselves a sizeable bonus at the end of that year. The second was an attempt in 1934 to force employees to contribute to Republican candidate Merriam's campaign for governor of California against the Democratic and Epic candidate, Upton Sinclair. (The studios also made propaganda inserts for newsreels to show the "devastating" effect of socialism that would follow Sinclair's election). Most disturbing, at least to the writers in 1936—a time when I was employed at MGM—was the attempt of the studio brass, notably Irving Thalberg (in a harsh personal appearance before all of us who were duly assembled in his MGM projection room), to warn of the dire consequences of unionization, an event which will be chronicled in greater detail in the chapter on unions.

There were many physical changes at the studio during the thirties. Some, as indicated, were caused by the introduction of sound, most notably the soundproofed shooting stages demanded by the sound experts imported from the East. One stage housed a theater set that was used principally for musicals but, if it was redressed, could serve as the locale for a political meeting. It had a fully equipped stage and an orchestra pit, but only ten rows of orchestra seats and only one side with balcony and loge boxes. The other side was open—as was true of many sets. After all, there had to be a place for the camera and crew.

In 1936, the MGM management decided to build a new commissary, so while construction was under way that summer, the lunchtime operation was moved to a large tent on the lawn in front of the dressing rooms, which stretched for about two hundred yards along Washington Boulevard. The back of the dressing rooms formed the street wall of the studio on Washington Boulevard, so there were no windows. On the studio side, there were walkways stretching the entire length of each floor of the two-story wooden structure. This was before the days when stars demanded their own trailers to follow them from location to location, but the leading players had larger dressing rooms than the newcomers and were given space closer to the main service areas for make-up and hair-dressing.

Marion Davies was the first performer at MGM to have a bungalow of her own. It was constructed adjacent to, and slightly in front of, the communal dressing rooms. She was, after all, the darling of newspaper tycoon William Randolph Hearst, whose Cosmopolitan Films, some of which featured Miss Davies, were distributed through MGM. It was a useful affiliation for the studio because of the favorable press that was assured in Hearst papers across the country. And it lasted until 1934 when Norma Shearer, wife of Irving Thalberg, was promised a role that Hearst wanted for Marion Davies—that of Marie Antoinette in the film of the same name. Shearer had already been given the role of Elizabeth Barrett in *The Barretts of Wimpole Street*, another dramatic role that Hearst wanted for Marion.

Convinced that Shearer would get all the roles he wanted for Marion Davies, Hearst moved Cosmopolitan Films to Warner Bros. and Davies' bungalow (a rather large little manse of fifteen rooms) was moved from Culver City to Warners' Burbank studio at the same time.

Davies's studio bungalow set the pattern for other persons of importance to follow. When Irving Thalberg returned from twelve months of recuperation from his heart attack (some of which was spent at the spa of Bad Nauheim in Germany), he decided to head up his own independent unit and moved out of his office next to my father into a new bungalow that was built just for him and his staff. He had his own chef and dining room, and many of his close associates, including my father, chose to eat with him rather than in the executive dining room in the commissary.

Commissaries at all of the studios were interesting gathering places where a lot of studio and personal business transpired. Previews were reported and discussed, union organization was plotted, clients met with agents to whine about assignments and salaries, and one could always tell which features were in production by spotting the bit players who went to lunch in their make-up and costumes.

At MGM, there were at least two large tables reserved for specific clienteles—a directors' table and a writers' table. The directors' table was in the center of the room and, in addition to the Woody Van Dykes, Bob Leonards, and Jack Conways, it attracted heads of departments and a few composers, as well as some of the higher priced writers who identified with management. Anyone could join the group, but in doing so one took a chance of having to pay the tab for everyone there. A chuckaluck basket at one end of the table was turned by each of the eaters, with the low man paying for the lot but eating free for the rest of the week. The conversation at the writers' table was more union- than company-oriented and there were more laughs. As the struggle between the studios and the Screen Writers Guild heated up from 1936 onward, the two tables became, in fact, rival camps.

Management sought to keep employees together as one happy family. The commissary was the gathering place, although back lot workers seldom ate there. They brought their lunches and used the commissary for an occasional snack or cup of coffee. But all studio activities were announced on a bulletin board in the eating place. And when a studio-wide golf tournament was in the offing, the prizes (quite lavish, since they were donated principally by the studio's suppliers of goods and services) were put on display near the cash registers. There were baseball games almost every Sunday on a real diamond left over from a 1920s William Haines production, *Slide Kelly Slide*. Buster Keaton, a baseball maniac, organized these and, if I recall correctly, played second base for the home team.

Though there was pretense of maintaining a democratic atmosphere, most socializing was distinctly segregated. The studio was a male-dominated community, and the barber shop which adjoined the commissary was the *agora* of male activity. This is where Rudy, the bootlegger, plied his trade and, after the repeal of Prohibition, took bets on horses running on tracks across the country.

In the early thirties, the studio had a six-day work week, but on Saturday mornings in the fall, the barber shop was a veritable betting parlor for wagers on college football games. And those producers, directors, and writers who were not directly involved in production on any given Saturday would take off for the Los Angeles Coliseum to watch USC or UCLA take on an invading eleven. Some of those games, especially at the start of the season, were very one-sided as USC mopped up on Occidental or Whittier. But most barber shop betting involved giving or taking points.

Budd Schulberg and I thought we were pigskin experts and liked to get involved with the betting crowd. Like the barber shop habitués, we were sports crazy. In addition to our own nickel bets on as many as fifty Saturday college football games, including such little known teams as Slippery Rock and Ball State, we would often travel a couple of hundred miles to Fresno or Bakersfield for track meets—high school or college. Athletes on Southern California high school track teams were then good enough for the Olympics: There were Darby Jones, the greyish-black high jumper from L.A. Polytechnic; Frank Wykoff, the sprinter from Glendale High; and Cornelius Johnson, from L.A. High, who actually won a gold medal. L.A. High also had a sterling sprinter who could match strides with Wykoff. His name was Frank Lombardi and his brother Vince was a major league ball-player.

The studio brass were big fans, too, and they often bet large sums. Yet they also liked to fraternize with coaches and star athletes. Almost everyone knows the story of John Wayne who was "discovered" while playing football for the University of Southern California (USC) under his real name of Marion Morrison. Other actors who graduated from the local playing fields were Ward Bond, Woody Strode, and Kenny Washington. Ferris Webster, a USC half-miler, became a film editor, as did Cotton Warburton, an SC quarterback. Jesse Hibbs, a tackle and USC football team captain, worked for many years as an assistant director, as did Russ Saunders who was famous for running back a kick for seventy-six yards against Notre Dame. And one of the big success stories was that of Aaron Rosenberg, a USC All-American guard, who started as an assistant director and rose through the ranks after World War II to become a major producer. (In this, he may have been helped by his brother, the talent agent Frank Rosenberg.)

The Rose Bowl game was a major event for the sports aficionados, and I can remember two occasions when the MGM bigwigs hired a bus, complete with bar and good food, to transport about twenty of us to Pasadena. The bus could not beat the horrendous traffic on Colorado Boulevard, but the delays were relatively painless in that gin-soaked atmosphere.

The only nighttime studio party I ever attended was at the Biltmore Hotel in downtown Los Angeles. It was a fancy, black-tie affair and was limited to the upper echelon of studio personnel. Entertainment was provided by tyros in the studio stock company, with Judy Garland's rendition of the teary "Dear Mr. Gable" being a show stopper. She repeated this number on screen in *The Broadway Melody of 1938,* but my recollection is that she was used primarily as an entertainer at studio affairs during her first years at the studio.

The studio actually had two child vocalists under contract in 1936, the year I went to work there as a junior writer. One was Garland, who sang pop stuff; the other was Deanna Durbin, a coloratura soprano who could do arias from operas and operettas. I remember going to the commissary one day with my collaborator, Richard Maibaum (who was later responsible for writing almost all the James Bond movies) and finding it so crowded that we were put at a table with two youngsters whom I knew to be Garland and Durbin. Deanna, pretty and slim, was having an ice cream soda while the overweight Judy was having a milkshake. Lapping up the rich goodies, they talked mostly about dieting.

Durbin and Garland made one short together at MGM. It was called *Every Sunday* and probably had a slight story, but all I remember about it is that each did her thing at a park bandstand to local applause. The brass at the studio was in a quandary. They couldn't figure out how to use both girls. Garland, for some reason, was favored by L. B. Mayer despite her plump figure and slightly piglike face. But she did have a sensational way with a popular song. So Durbin's contract was not renewed. Universal signed her and made her an instant star in *100 Men and a Girl,* which was about a little Miss Fix-It who induces Leopold Stokowski to conduct an orchestra of unemployed musicians, including Adolphe Menjou, Deanna's violinist father, at which concert Deanna is the soloist.

There were, of course, many parties ~~that were held~~ in private homes, including ours. In the early days—the silent twenties—these parties almost always included gag films that were made at the studio especially for these occasions. They usually poked fun at the more prominent guests, boss L. B. Mayer excepted. Well-known actors such as Lew Cody and Bea Lillie sometimes appeared in these "home movies," and the printed gags were written by the studio's leading title writers, Joe Farnham and Al Boasberg.

I didn't see many of these. When the parties were held at my house, I was sent out of the projection room because the films were consid-

ered too risqué for a twelve-year-old. Once I did sneak into the projection booth to see what the fuss was about. If it was naughty, it was over
my head. There was one film about the kidnapping of Aimee Semple
McPherson, played by Beatrice Lillie, in which she is rescued by the
MGM lion. And another had a redundant series of credits that made
fun of director Bob Leonard, whose mysterious middle initial was simply the letter "Z." "Produced by Robert Zipp Leonard, directed by
Robert Zapp Leonard, edited by Robert Zack Leonard, *with* Robert
Zero Leonard," and so forth. The movie, introduced by some titles,
then consisted of a series of dissolves from close shots of some of the
guests (who obviously had no idea why the shots were made) to what
was supposed to be their metaphoric images. A shot of hypochondriac
producer Hunt Stromberg dissolved to a hot water bottle, for example;
studio manager Eddie Mannix dissolved to a bulldog who looked just
like him; and director Jack Conway became a horse's rear end. I didn't
think these comparisons were very funny, but the guests did.

I actually appeared in one of the party gag reels, and my father had
the original 35-millimeter print transferred to 16-millimeter so I still
have the two-minute joke. It begins with a title, "A Look into the Future." We then see Irving Thalberg and Harry Rapf asleep on the
bench in what was easily recognizable as their waiting room. Cut to
Thalberg's Office. I get up from behind his desk, a twelve-year-old in
shirt sleeves, take one of Thalberg's gold-tipped cigarettes out of the
box on the glass topped desk, put on a straw hat, and go out the rear
door to the balcony and down the steps to the street below. I am approached by an obsequious man in a Norfolk jacket, who hands me
a paper to sign. The man is director Mervyn LeRoy, slightly stooped
over because of apparent old age. I sign and proceed to the curb where
Thalberg's limousine is waiting. Thalberg's chauffeur, Slickem, de-
crepit and grey, opens the door for me. Cut to *the Back Seat of the
Limo.* Pretty actress Marie Prevost is waiting for me. She hasn't aged.

There were lots of shenanigans like this in the old studio, but I cannot leave this description of the studio without a mention of morals,
the alleged lack of which has given Hollywood an unsavory reputation since the first move west. As David Halberstam says in his book
The Fifties, there was "an endless stream of young women who had
been voted the best-looking girls in their high school classes and who
thereupon went to Hollywood and queued up at Schwab's Drug
Store, hoping to be discovered." When it didn't happen—as it had
with the real-life Lana Turner or with the fictional Janet Gaynor in *A*

Star Is Born—the women allegedly went downtown and found less glamorous ways to make a living.

The truth was, however, that the studios had more efficient ways to locate talent. And the so-called talent scouts, who roamed the country looking at promising young actresses and actors, at singers and dancers, as well as at comely cheerleaders, were, for good reason, a rather puritanical lot. Ivan Kahn was the talent scout at 20th Century–Fox when I worked there, and he and his wife, Jessie, felt a protective responsibility toward the pretty young girls they signed up for Fox pictures. On the other hand, they felt obliged to see to it that the girls were introduced to nice young men. I was, for a time, lucky to be one of them.

I was once invited to the Kahns' to meet three newcomers whom he was most enthusiastic about. They were Linda Darnell, Mary Healy, and Doris Bowden. Linda was the great beauty. She was also the youngest—maybe thirteen—and she wore a prim blue velvet dress with a white lace collar and, believe it or not, white bobby socks. She was a bit too "developed" to play adolescents and much too young to be a leading lady, so the studio, as I recall, sent her home for a couple of years to mature. By the mid-forties she was Fox's sexiest star. Mary Healey was probably the most talented of the lot. She could dance and sing and mimic and was used in some of the Fox musicals. But she made her biggest splash years later on radio or TV—I can't remember which—in a comedy family act with her husband, Peter Lind Hayes. Doris Bowden was attractive but no beauty. She was the oldest, had finished two years of college, and seemed to be the most intellectual, so I asked for a date and went out with her several times. She played minor roles, usually as a serious, introspective daughter or sister. One such part was as Rose of Sharon in *The Grapes of Wrath*. The next news I had of her was that she had married the writer-producer of that film, Nunnally Johnson, and that she retired from acting, as far as I know, and stayed married to him until he died in 1977.

I had the good fortune in 1931 to write a story that was used as the basis for a youth movie starring Jackie Cooper (who had become a star playing the movie role of a cartoon kid known as "Skippy"). My movie was called *Divorce in the Family.* The screenplay was written by Delmer Daves (who would some day be a noted director) and dealt with Cooper's difficulty in adjusting to his mother's remarriage (to Conrad Nagel) and to his older brother's sudden interest in girls. I mention this only to explain why the movie had a number of big scenes of high school affairs—picnics, proms, and the like—requiring dozens of attractive teenage extras of both sexes. One had only to visit the set of *Divorce in the Family* to meet most of the attractive young people in Hollywood. And as the coauthor of the original story, I had a built-in introduction to a bevy of nice girls.

The female lead in this film—the heartthrob of Cooper's brother (played by Maurice Murphy)—was Jean Parker, a girl I thought to be sixteen and later discovered to be twenty. She was making her first screen appearance, having been signed to a contract by L. B. Mayer's close associate and (thought by some to be) his political hatchet woman, Ida Koverman. When I wanted a date with Jean, I had to clear it with Mrs. Koverman. She seemed to be not only Parker's discoverer but also her duenna. I was given a strict set of rules, not the least of which was that I was under no circumstances to drink and ~~that~~ I was to have Jean home at ten o'clock. Jean was a wonderful, lively, and intelligent girl and is perhaps best remembered for her work as one of Katharine Hepburn's sisters in *Little Women*. Several years later, after she had married a handsome young man named George MacDonald, who was finishing up his B.A. at UCLA, she gave me a slim volume of Edna St. Vincent Millay's verse play, *Aria de Capo,* inscribed by Jean, "To someone who will know why I love this." After she left Hollywood in the early forties, she had a fairly successful career on Broadway and in stock. She went back to movies in the fifties, mostly in supporting roles; the last one I recall was a real clinker about venereal disease called *Stigma* in 1972.

Those were some of the more wholesome and innocent aspects of the studio dating game. But sometimes the best of intentions went awry. I remember wanting a date with a gorgeous extra and finding out ~~that~~ she was working in a garden party scene for *As You Desire Me,* a Garbo film, which meant the set was closed. So I wrote a note, asking to meet the girl in the wardrobe department (my uncle's bailiwick) when shooting stopped for the day. I gave the note to the assistant director, a friend of mine named Red Golden, and, though he did indeed give the note to the girl and I did meet her, he also shared its contents with most of the crew members, so ~~that~~ it got around that the boss's son was using his position to make out with extras.

Being exposed to so many beautiful young women was, in some ways, more than a susceptible young man could be expected to endure with equanimity. And the truth is that I and most of my friends not only dated the girls who worked as extras or had bit parts in movies, but we married them as well. These young women were a far cry from the "dumb blonde" image of starlets one reads about in fan magazines.

I met my wife, Louise, on a blind date. She was working as a skater in a Sonja Henie picture at Fox, and one of our mutual friends, also skating but married to my friend Budd Schulberg, played Cupid. Louise worked all day, turning over most of her pay to her mother, and went to school at night. She was still going to school—actually auditing classes—in her seventies while I was teaching at Dartmouth. So much for the "dumb blonde" stereotype!

And now for an answer to the frequently asked question, do I really think the movies of the thirties are better than those made today?

Chapter 4

Hollywood's Golden Years

Were movies better yesterday than today? When I say "yes," I have to qualify my answer because I am obviously talking about a select few of those old movies that have survived the test of time—which is, after all, one measure of artistic achievement. We look at contemporary work en masse, and there are, of course, a few films every year (even in the dismal output of today) that may still be viewed with some interest fifty years from now. I don't think it will be *Pulp Fiction* or *Jurassic Park,* two of the recent big grossers, but I still hope to find a worthy successor to *It Happened One Night* or *Modern Times.*

There were five thousand films made in the decade of the thirties. We see only a few—which may be just as well. In the old days, we saw them under all kinds of conditions: sometimes in fancy movie palaces with stage shows as prologues; sometimes in second-run neighborhood theaters with banko and keno and giveaway dishes; sometimes on Saturday afternoons with a full program of short subjects, including the weekly chapter of a serial that might run as long as twelve weeks. There was always a newsreel, often a travelogue, and after a while some audiences demanded double features.

Where I went to college in Hanover, New Hampshire, the local movie house ran at least four different movies a week. Admission was twenty-five cents. And many of us saw four movies a week. What were some of my favorite movies at that time? Social dramas topped the list: *All Quiet on the Western Front, The Informer, The Life of Emile Zola, I am a Fugitive From a Chain Gang, They Won't Forget, Fury.* Comedies: anything with the Marx Brothers or Charlie Chaplin but especially *Horsefeathers* and *City Lights.* And the screwballs—*It Happened One Night, My Man Godfrey, Trouble in Paradise.* I could name

59

a dozen more. Think of the great gangster movies and you come up with *Little Caesar, Scarface,* and *The Public Enemy.* Think of suspense and I recall the great Hitchcock British thrillers tinged with comedy—*The Thirty-Nine Steps* and *The Lady Vanishes.* And the U.S. horror films, *Dracula* and *Frankenstein.*

If musicals were your forte—though they weren't mine—this was also the decade that introduced the Astaire-Rogers series, the backstage girlie shows of Busby Berkeley, and the first few all-star Broadway Melodies with the MGM musical stock company of Judy Garland, Eleanor Powell, Buddy Ebsen, Ann Miller, and eventually Gene Kelly.

In my youth, the movies seemed to offer us role models. I can't say the models were all good, but they were mythic. And the subject matter itself, inevitably escapist, took us into worlds we would never inhabit ourselves. Whether it was the underworld, the world of the very rich and powerful, the world of the future, or the unlimited aspects of the past, the movies broadened our horizons. To some extent, they still do and when I see movies such as *Farewell, My Concubine* or Berri's *Germinal* I am not only entertained, but I learn something about the world we live in or the world of the past.

The industry in the thirties had to come to grips with a new technology—sound. Today's faster, sophisticated film stocks, wide-screen cameras, and lightweight portable recording equipment had yet to be fully developed. But it was a period when an enormous amount of product had to be turned out, and the studios were rich enough to attract and develop fascinating personalities and to shape a variety of stories to fit their talents.

Movies became the great popular entertainment form for the masses, with something for everyone. But with mass popularity came the possibility of influencing behavior and opinion, and a counter-reaction arose to ensure that this influence was kept under control. Pressure from outside sources that attempted to affect the content of movies began on a national scale in the twenties, partly because film stars were being exploited as sex objects and partly because studio publicity mills were using fan magazines and gossip columns to exploit the private lives of its celebrities. Hollywood became known as a city of sin, and when several major scandals received national coverage—the Fatty Arbuckle case, the William Desmond Taylor murder, the Wally Reid drug charges—the industry set up its own self-policing body to avoid local and statewide censorship and boycotts of its films. Pressure was coming from religious and moral crusading groups, much as it was brought to bear a few years ago on MCA/Universal for *The Last Temptation of Christ.*

In the twenties, the industry named a former postmaster general as its so-called czar to deal with infractions of moral waywardness. His name was Will Hays and he introduced the first movie "code." But this was intended more to stop the pressure than to change the course of production.

The major crackdown on film content, however, came from outside sources in the early thirties and was provoked more than anything by the success of the films of Mae West. Her films were condemned from pulpits across the nation, even though they were clean as a whistle by today's standards and offered nothing more offensive than sexual innuendo. Such lines as "Come up and see me sometime," "When I'm good, I'm good, but when I'm bad, I'm better," "The finest lady who ever walked the streets," and so forth brought threats from a Catholic organization, the Legion of Decency, which included picketing and boycotts and were sufficiently strong for the movie industry to knuckle under and introduce a new production code, the administration of which they turned over to a representative of the Legion, Joseph Breen. He held this post as Administrator of the Code for at least twenty years.

From that point on, every script was submitted to the Code office for scrutiny before production. It was a self-censoring operation in order to head off censorship on state and local levels. And sexual innuendo was not its only target. Offensive language was taboo. One could not say "Jesus" or "Lord," except in a religious context. "Damn" and "Hell" were excluded—an exception being made for Rhett Butler's famous exit line "I don't give a damn" in *Gone with the Wind.* Overt prostitution or homosexuality could not be shown or referred to in dialogue. Husbands and wives could not be shown sharing the same bed. Kisses had to be discreet. Nudity was, of course, excluded, although it had never been shown extensively in American films. And in a reaction against the glorification of the gangster— who, after all, provided one of the few examples of success during the depression— he not only had to die in the end (something he usually did anyway) but he had to be shown in an unfavorable light throughout. The Warner brothers, who had specialized in gangster films, immediately converted gangster heroes like Edward G. Robinson and Jimmy Cagney into equally aggressive and trigger-happy law enforcement agents—as is evidenced in 1935's *G Man.*

Many of us thought ~~that~~ the code was too stringent and resented the blue pencils of the industry-paid censors. But while I do not condone censorship, I find that restrictions sometimes lead to ingeniously creative ways of accomplishing story-telling objectives—ways that are more satisfying and even more sexually suggestive, in some instances, than showing intimate relationships explicitly, as so many films do today. Two pairs of shoes—male and female—outside a hotel room door tells me pretty clearly what's going on inside. And when I see Asta, Nora's dog in *The Thin Man,* cover her eyes with her paws in an upper berth, I can guess what Nora and Nick Charles are up to down below. Language taboos, on the other hand, were sometimes very inhibiting for writers, although I am not altogether pleased with the current permissiveness toward gutter language, much of which is just downright ugly—and offensive when used repetitively as a form of characterization.

MGM followed most of the trends that were pursued by the industry as a whole, but, because L. B. Mayer was the man who dictated policy, it pursued some unique themes as well. There was usually an exaltation of the family in MGM movies and, indeed, there was a genuine turn from sin and violence to goodness and mother love as the decade drew to a close. After all, *Love Finds Andy Hardy* was the biggest hit of 1938 and Shirley Temple the number one female box-office star for several years before that. There were a host of child stars—most of them dominating wholesome, family-type entertainment—Freddie Bartholomew, Jackie Cooper, Mickey Rooney, the early Judy Garland, Jane Withers, Deanna Durbin, Dean Stockwell, Mitzi Green, Bobby Breen, and, of course, to fill in where adults fear to tread—as the child of glamorous leading ladies such as Marlene Dietrich in *Blonde Venus* and Ann Harding in *Gallant Lady*—the ubiquitous Dickie Moore.

In the early thirties, MGM—like all the other studios—had its full share of fallen women, beginning with Ruth Chatterton in *Madame X,* Helen Hayes in *The Sin of Madelon Claudet,* and of course Garbo in her first talkie, an adaptation of O'Neill's *Anna Christie.* Garbo was undoubtedly MGM's most important star in the early thirties. She was discovered by L. B. Mayer on a European jaunt, and he brought her to Hollywood with her patron and favorite director, Mauritz Stiller. Appearing first in silent films, she was always the "temptress" (indeed, that was the title of one of her films), but she had a Swedish accent and there was some question whether she could make the leap into talkies. She could.

Her first talkie in 1930 was ballyhooed—often above the title—with the great news: "GARBO SPEAKS." The subject was *Anna Christie*, based on a play by Eugene O'Neill in which she has been a prostitute and her problem is to convince her boyfriend (Charles Bickford) that her past was involuntary and certainly not enjoyable. Also in 1930 was *Romance,* in which Garbo is an opera singer with many wealthy men in her life but in love with an Episcopalian minister, whom she gives up for his own good in order to forestall his intention to forsake the cloth. The story is told by the minister in middle age to his grandson—a favorite device for stories of this sort. In *Inspiration,* based on Daudet's *Sappho*, she is a promiscuous Parisian model transformed by an idealistic young man whom she ultimately frees to go on with his diplomatic career while she marries a former lover.

Later she played the famous World War I spy Mata Hari, a role that could condone her promiscuity in the interest of her patriotic craft. In *Queen Christina,* made in 1933, her premarital sex is pursued for pleasure rather than economic gain and, as a queen (of Sweden), she is obviously immune from public reproach—but only up to a point, because she abdicates in the end. In most of her roles from then on—conforming to the code—she may have been a bit adulterous but was never a kept woman—except in the prototypical and much admired *Camille* in 1937. And she dies in that film.

So sex was still possible after the Code was instituted, but it had to be punished. And there were many subsidiary characters who continued to portray the old image of the prostitute with a heart of gold. There are two characters in *Dead End* (1936) who fill this bill. And then there was Belle Watling in *Gone with the Wind.* And Claire Trevor in a half dozen films—even getting her man (and winning an Oscar) in *Stagecoach.* Generally, the rule was that fallen women must suffer degradation—except that they did not in the films of Mae West and Ernst Lubitsch. Many of these women are portrayed as being of humble origin, and at one point in the story they attain not only wealth but the manner that goes with it. This is true of Garbo in *The Rise and Fall of Susan Lennox* and of Crawford in *Possessed.*

Feminists are quite aware that women in thirties movies usually had to pay the piper for leaving the straight and narrow, whereas the leading men could be charming rogues without paying too severe a penalty for their misdeeds. Films about gamblers and jewel thieves allowed for environments of luxury and splendor. Considering that since Americans were standing in lines at soup kitchens, the audience didn't feel much sympathy for the dowager or lady of leisure who is victimized by the heist of her diamond bracelet. The suave men like Bulldog Drummond and the protagonist in Michael Arlen's *The Falcon* (played by George Sanders) were just emulating Robin Hood—stealing from the rich to give to the poor. And if the jewel thief himself was short of change, who could fault him for lifting a bauble or two?

Some of Hollywood's most popular leading men played these roles as likeable scoundrels. And in the jewel thief category, women did pretty well, too. Norma Shearer was an elegant snatch artist, gowned by Adrian, in *The Last of Mrs. Cheyney.* Marlene Dietrich had a similar role in *Desire,* but she was reformed in the end by an upright but tolerant American, Gary Cooper. *Trouble in Paradise,* directed by Ernst Lubitsch from a script by Samson Raphaelson, is the epitome of this affectionate portrayal of petty thievery. Sin is not punished, nor is virtue rewarded.

I have already described some of the characteristics of the studio system in the early thirties. Most of my information is based on what I experienced at MGM in the first few years of sound when my father was riding high. I should not conclude this chapter on the thirties, however, without some reference to the evolution of credits. The familiar logo of the MGM lion was inherited from the Goldwyn studio. The caption "ars gratia artis" ("art for art's sake") was devised by Howard Dietz, the songwriter and longtime head of publicity in the New York office.

Here is a sample of the credits on one of my father's successful pictures—*Possessed* (1931).

Card 1

JOAN CRAWFORD
in Clarence Brown's Production
POSSESSED
with
Clark Gable

Card 2

From the stage play, "The Mirage"
by
Edgar Selwyn
Adaptation and Dialogue Continuity
by
Lenore Coffee

Recording Director	Douglas Shearer
Art Director	Cedric Gibbons
Gowns by	Adrian
Photography by	Oliver T. Marsh
Film Editor	William Levanway

Card 3—The cast.

And that was it! Note that Gable is second to Crawford at this time. His career was just beginning. He had appeared as a gangster with Norma Shearer in *A Free Soul.* There is no producer credit, as I mentioned previously. A few of the studio's directors—Clarence Brown, King Vidor, Victor Fleming, and Sidney Franklin—were important enough to receive the kind of credit Clarence Brown receives here. But he and everyone else at the studio knew that Harry Rapf was the producer, just as they knew that Irving Thalberg was the producer of all of Norma Shearer's pictures, even though his name does not appear. As for the rest of the credits, the names of Cedric Gibbons for art direction, Douglas Shearer for sound, and (later) Edwin Willis for set decoration are generic rather than specific. They were the heads of their respective departments and they did indeed approve the plans as prepared by their associates, but their names continue to appear on all MGM films throughout most of the thirties.

By the mid-thirties, the number of credits—all of which preceded rather than followed the movie—had increased noticeably. On *Dinner at Eight* in 1933, David Selznick got credit as producer. One reason—Selznick, then L. B. Mayer's son-in-law, had his own unit. People often referred to the Selznick ascendancy at the studio with a variation on the title of Ernest Hemingway's famous novel: "The Son-in-Law Also Rises."

On a 1937 movie, *Test Pilot,* we find the writers having a card of their own and we find new credits for "musical score by," "special effects," and "montage effects." The final caption, following the cast, says: "The events and characters depicted in this photoplay are fictitious. Any similarity to persons living or dead is purely coincidental." That short disclaimer, first introduced in 1935, was the consequence of the famous *Rasputin* libel case which cost MGM several hundred thousand dollars when they were sued by a New York lawyer named Fannie Holtzman on behalf of Prince and Princess Yousoupoff, bona fide members of the Romanoff court, who, though presumed dead, were still living in London. Though some of the actual names of the czar's family had been changed in the movie, the identity of Princess Y. was unmistakable, and since the movie's princess was shown as one of the monk's rape victims—and the real-life princess denied that such an outrage had ever occurred—the British court had the distinct pleasure of slapping a hefty financial penalty on a major U.S. company.

Think of MGM as the glamour studio. Even so, the biggest moneymaker of 1930 was that studio's *Min and Bill*, about a couple of lowlifes on the waterfront, for which Marie Dressler won an Academy Award. A year later MGM's biggest moneymaker was a tearjerker called *The Champ*, for which Wallace Beery won an Oscar as a boozy overweight prizefighter with an adoring son, played by Jackie Cooper. The script, by Frances Marion, also won an Oscar. *Min and Bill*, *The Champ*, and *Tugboat Annie*, the 1933 sequel to *Min and Bill*, were all produced by my father. *The Champ* was directed by King Vidor, a director whose name is preserved in the annals of movie history to this day. *Min and Bill* was directed by George Hill, the husband of writer Frances Marion and just as well known as Vidor in the early thirties but, because of his untimely death in 1934, virtually unknown today.

I mention this to emphasize the weakness of film history as we know it—the fact that most film historians latch onto the same limited list of directors as examples of those who rose above the commercial strictures of a mass-market industry. But there were many others, especially in the thirties, who, because they didn't survive long enough to be extolled in the age of personal press-agentry, are now virtually forgotten. They were in great demand in their day and produced superlative work. We see and appreciate their movies, but they will remain in historical limbo until film scholars of the future pick up the biographical pieces—which, because information about movies was not considered worthy of academic interest and thus not adequately preserved in the thirties, will not be too easy. Here is a partial list of more or less forgotten directors (for scholars to dabble in): Monta Bell, Herbert Brenon, William Nigh, George Archainbaud, Rex Ingram, Gregory La Cava, Frank Lloyd, George Fitzmaurice, and, last but not least, the winner of two of the first three Academy Awards (for *Two Arabian Nights* and *All Quiet on the Western Front*), Lewis Milestone.

It is very hard to convey what Hollywood in the thirties was really like. Hollywood was coming of age; it went from being a youthful and adventurous frontier town where making movies seemed like a lot of fun to being a manufacturing town with a sobering recognition of its place in the corporate and political world. It was affected internally by the growth of unions and by the influx of hard-nosed business types from the East, representing capital; it was also affected externally by threats of censorship and government anti-trust action, by congressional political attacks, ultimately by TV, and by the consequences of the blacklist which it imposed on itself. It could never again function as an apparently happy family.

Chapter 5

My Trip to the USSR

One might think that an account of a college junior's trip to the Soviet Union in 1934 has nothing to do with growing up in Hollywood. In some ways, that is correct. But the reader must know something about that trip to understand why I, the son of a bigshot movie producer and in line for an executive's job at his father's studio, decided to turn my back on that kind of career in favor of membership in the Communist Party.

In the spring of 1934 I was a junior at Dartmouth College, and there appeared on the bulletin board in Robinson Hall (then the student activity building) a notice that said, "Summer study in the USSR—$325—all inclusive round trip." The notice went on to explain that the trip was sponsored by the National Students League (a left-wing organization). The group would leave by ship from New York to England, transfer to a Soviet ship for the second leg of the journey to Leningrad, travel by train to Moscow, spend six weeks of study at the Anglo-American Institute, and then make a choice between various ten-day tours to interesting sections of the USSR, followed by a return to Moscow and two weeks as guests of Soviet students, at which time the fall theater season would have begun. It was the last item that was especially intriguing to me. The possibility of attending the Soviet theater—the Moscow Art, the Vakhtangov, the Meyerhold—which was considered one of the most exciting in the world, was not only intriguing but made it possible for me to convince my father (who would do anything to enhance my education as a potential movie producer) that a trip to a Communist country might have some value. He came to regret his approval, but I went.

It turned out that there would be five other Dartmouth undergraduates—my roommate, Budd Schulberg; Bobby Boehm, son of a prominent New York City judge; Raphael Silverman, son of the only Jewish professor at Dartmouth and later to gain fame as a violist under the adopted name of Raphael Hillyer; John Spiegel, a senior and one of the heirs apparent of the Spiegel family of Chicago, known for their mail order catalog; and Charlie Strauss, who was a senior and the most dedicated Marxist of the lot. (Later, when he became a succcessful advertising executive, he turned out to be the most conservative.) Another Dartmouth undergraduate who turned up in Moscow was Buster May, heir to the owners of the May Department stores and later to date many starlets in Hollywood. Our group, which was joined by male students from Yale, Harvard, and Princeton and women from Wellesley, Smith, and Vassar may have been the first group of U.S. undergraduates to study in Russia since the October Revolution of 1917, and we were certainly pioneers in what is now a fairly standard practice of college foreign study.

One of FDR's first acts as president had been to reestablish formal diplomatic ties with the Soviet Union. He sent one of his buddies, an aristocratic Philadelphian, William C. Bullitt, to Moscow as ambassador. *The New York Times* Moscow correspondent, whose dispatches we had read and who was to write a friendly book about the Soviets, was Walter Duranty.

We thought at first that the Anglo-American Institute was set up to accomodate the expected invasion of U.S. students, though it may have been in existence before we came, to handle British, Canadian and English-speaking Chinese young people who made up about half the student body. This experiment in education lasted one more year—through 1935—and then, because of deteriorating relations between the United States and the USSR, it ceased—as far as Americans were concerned. But it was fun while it lasted, and if I am to be judged as an example, it served the Soviet purpose of converting U.S. youth to a pro-Communist point of view. This does not mean that all of us joined the Party. Some, I am sure, never did. Others, like me, became Soviet boosters when we got home and were eventually recruited to the Party itself.

Why? In my case, there were three reasons. One, although the Soviet standard of living was far below that in the United States, there were basic socialist features making it appear that a planned economy in a workers' state could eventually provide, according to the idealistic Marxist principle, "to each according to his needs, from each according to his ability." We knew that this idea was not an immediate prospect. In fact, the Communist bureaucracy had already found that workers failed to perform at maximum efficiency without the promise of special rewards. Hence, the "Stakhanovite" system, whereby a worker (the first was actually a man named Stakhanov) received something material in addition to medals for high standards of effort and efficiency.

But I was impressed that there was education for all, that illiteracy was being drastically reduced, and that students were given a stipend while they attended school and were guaranteed jobs on graduation—whether from high school or the university. To those of us who were children of the capitalist depression and very insecure about future employment, such job insurance seemed utopian. The management of factories, schools, and social services was in the hands of the people themselves and, like the collective farms, at least the ones we saw, seemed to be run on a democratic basis. Or so we believed at the time.

The second reason for my pro-Soviet attitude started out as a negative. Most progressive U.S. undergraduates were pacifists, and Russia seemed to have an undue number of men (and women) in uniform. Why such a big army if it was a country dedicated to peace, as they claimed? The reason given was the threat of fascism, especially as evidenced by the rise of Hitler in Nazi Germany. One striking poster (in socialist realism style) showed a villainous-looking Nazi outside the wall of what looked like a Soviet Garden of Eden. An enlarged, disembodied fist loomed high over the wall from the Soviet side and the caption read, "Keep your Nazi snout out of our Soviet garden." (I bought a copy of that poster and had it among my belongings as I returned from Kiev to the Atlantic coast by train. When we crossed the German border, German customs started checking the contents of baggage. I tossed the poster out of the train window—along with other anti-Nazi propaganda I had purchased in Russia and wanted to take home.)

Thus, I came to the conclusion that the Red Army was strictly an army of defense and that the Soviet Union was the one country in the world that called attention to the menace of Hitler and the Nazis, who were already making threats of world domination and were denouncing Jews as the cause of all the world's problems. That leads to the third reason for my pro-Soviet attitude, which may seem a little preposterous today in view of the frequent charges of anti-Semitism in Russia. Believe it or not, in 1934 anti-Semitism was actually a crime in the USSR. It was punishable by imprisonment. Yiddish theaters thrived in all the major cities and a separate Jewish republic—Birobidzhan—

Chapter 5

had been created where Yiddish was the official language. (Many of us disapproved of the Birobidzhan settlement as a kind of ghetto, but remember that there had been a lot of clamor for a Jewish state and in 1934 there was worldwide Zionism but no Israel.)

We knew that Judaism as a religion was frowned upon, if not outlawed. So was the formerly dominant Greek Orthodox Church. Many of the ornate tulip-domed churches had been turned into antireligious museums and the hitherto clandestine monks' quarters exposed as havens of corruption and debauchery. But it was an odd incident on a streetcar that answered most of our misgivings about Soviet anti-Semitism once and for all. Several of us had gone off on our own to explore the city. On this day, we were lost. Though none of our group spoke Russian, two of us spoke German and we had learned a trick to make our needs understood: look for someone who might be Jewish and familiar with Yiddish and speak to him in German.

Trying to spot someone who "looked Jewish" was, of course, an act of anti-Semitism in itself. But it usually worked. In this case, however, putting the question in German about how to get to the location of the Anglo-American Institute produced a tirade in bastard Yiddish. "Speak Yiddish," the man who looked Jewish shouted, "Speak Yiddish." When our German-speaking pair explained that they could not, he became even more vociferous and broke into English, "Speak Yiddish," he shouted. "This is the Soviet Union. It's not a crime to speak Yiddish."

We were convinced by this that anti-Semitism really was against Soviet policy. So was prostitution, though at least one American we met who was working for the Soviets said that he knew where obliging ladies could be found. (One of the principal arguments used by folks at home to challenge our favorable impressions was to say that we "only saw what they wanted us to see." We did see "what they wanted us to see," but we were never restricted from seeing anything else except by our lack of Soviet money and we were always given a few kopecks to get around on public transportation.)

The living standards for working people seemed to us appalling but, as young intellectuals, we were impressed by the fact that writers and artists and others with a cultural bent were, at this time, given special rewards in terms of living quarters and an occasional car. We happened to be in Moscow in the fall of 1934 for what was billed as the International Writers Congress. The Soviets were making a desperate attempt to reach writers all over the world, and one publication—*Soviet Literature*—was published in at least three foreign languages, including English.

A few of us went to the Writers' Congress on the day ~~that~~ the country's most famous writer, Maxim Gorky, was to speak. Though we had no headphones for translation, we were impressed by the attention given to literary culture. It is worth mentioning that one of our teachers at the Institute was Alexis Tolstoy, a descendant of the great Russian writer, and he, in English, had given us an introduction to the works of Sholokhov, Ehrenburg, and Mayakovsky.

None of this rather positive description of what we saw should lead readers to believe ~~that~~ the Soviet Union was actually a "free" state. We were perfectly aware of dictatorial rule and of bureaucracy at every lower level and thought we understood why it was necessary in order to make a transition to a democratic socialist society. One of the big arguments we had with our Soviet hosts and with some of the pro-Soviet Americans who lived in the USSR had to do with what we regarded as the impossibility of changing human nature. How could people ever accept such an idealistic principle as "To each according to his needs, from each according to his ability?" The dyed-in-the-wool Communists thought it could come about in a generation. And we hoped they were right.

In the meantime, we had to observe and face society as it was. And one of the chief problems we faced was how to get along without money. On the official exchange, which was the only one we were allowed to use, a dollar could be exchanged for one ruble and thirteen kopecks. If we went to the Park of Culture and Rest at night and wanted a soft drink, it would cost five rubles; admission to a movie was ten. We couldn't afford to buy anything or pay admission to anything.

Then, one Sunday night in the Moscow Park of Culture and Rest, we saw that they were playing an American movie, *Cabin in the Cotton,* with Bette Davis and Richard Barthelmess. I had seen the movie—it was about sharecroppers in the south—and I thought it would be fun to see it with a Soviet audience who would be reading subtitles while we understood the English dialogue. But there were three of us and we certainly did not have thirty rubles or even the nearly thirty dollars it would take to get thirty rubles. I decided to try a different ploy.

I went to the ticket counter, explained in feeble Russian that we were "trey Amerikanski studenti" and laid a U.S. dollar bill before the lady attendant. She smiled and beckoned for me to follow her to a spot somewhere behind her booth. There she gave me three tickets and thirty rubles in change. I was into the black market. Later that night, after the movie, we went to a restaurant with our thirty rubles and, for the first time, could afford to buy some drinks. But when the bill came for twenty rubles (which we could have paid) we repeated the scam, gave the waiter a dollar and he gave us another batch of rubles in change.

Thereafter, when shady characters approached us as we were leaving the post office downtown and showed us rolls of rubles and spoke of dollars, we would ask, "Skolke?" meaning "how much?" If the exchange seemed equitable, we would follow this creep for a few blocks, step into a doorway or a dark alley, and exchange dollars for rubles. The money gave us the freedom to go wherever we wanted, even to buy a few books, posters, pamphlets, and souvenirs. We knew we were playing with fire, that we could be thrown out of the country if caught. We also knew that most foreigners were doing what we were doing, that the fair value of the ruble was about a nickel—not eighty-seven cents, and that, until the Soviets changed the official exchange rate (which they ultimately did) the black market would continue.

Incidentally, our admission to *Cabin in the Cotton* provided another interesting insight into Soviet thought control. Having seen the movie, I knew the plot: the son of a sharecropper (Barthelmess) falls in love with Bette Davis, the daughter of the plantation owner. Barthelmess finds himself in a bind when the sharecroppers decide to go on strike against the owner for better conditions. Barthelmess sticks with his family and confronts the owner, father of his girlfriend, with the sharecroppers' demands. End of love affair, at least for the time being. The conclusion of the movie was a reconciliation and a love fest between sharecroppers and owners. What we saw in the Soviet theater was that movie, all right, but only up to a point! After sharecropper Barthelmess denounced the owner and broke off with Bette, the lights went up. Intermission, right? No—wrong. That was it! The sharecroppers had revolted against their exploiters! That was the Soviet version of *Cabin in the Cotton*!

Our Soviet trip ended in Kiev, from which we took a train to Warsaw and then had the choice of proceeding directly west across the south of Europe or northwest, which meant passing through Germany. Three of us—Schulberg, my cousin Al Mannheimer from Yale, and I—opted for Germany and planned a stopover for five days in Berlin. As Jews, fully aware of the Nazi's official policy of anti-Semitism, we knew this was slightly foolhardy, but we were curious.

We had only one person to contact—the manager of Warner

Bros.' Berlin office, a Jew whom I will call Manny Levy. All of the other film companies that were controlled by Jews had closed up shop—whether for safety's sake or because they were coerced, I don't know. If Manny was still there, it was because he had a beautiful Aryan girlfriend, Inga, and he knew that once he left he might never see her again. (We heard later that he left Berlin six weeks after we did. Al Mannheimer saw Inga in New York several years later. She was married to a German and had no idea what had happened to "Manny.")

But our stay in Berlin, with its display of ominous swastikas, its many pictures of Hitler, with brownshirts to be seen everywhere, with anti-Semitic magazines like *Juden* featured on newsstands and Jewish stars painted on the storefronts of closed shops, was in sharp contrast to the relaxed and friendly atmosphere we had enjoyed in Moscow. (There were no concentration camps at this time, so far as we knew, and many Jews with sufficient wherewithal had already emigrated or were planning to do so.) Manny maintained his contacts with what was left of the Jewish community. We would walk three blocks out of our way to ride with one of the few Jewish taxi drivers who was still working in the city. We ate in places where a few Jews were still employed, including one delicatessen where we were inhibited from having an open conversation—even in English—by the presence of a blackshirt (SS man) eating a pastrami sandwich at an adjacent table. (This was the latter half of September 1934, and I later realized that the infamous Nuremberg Congress, featured in Leni Riefenstahl's *Triumph of the Will,* was in fact taking place at that very time.)

The only mass display of National Socialist rule that we witnessed was the Sunday parade of brownshirts down the Unter den Linden. We were warned by Manny to stay away unless we were prepared to raise our hands in the Nazi salute when the swastika went by. People who didn't do the "Heil Hitler" bit when the flag went by were usually beaten on the spot, he said. We went, we didn't raise our hands, and nothing happened. We were stupid, but we were also lucky. And seeing that ominous parade was worth the risk: all of those odious characters, half of them with Hitler moustaches, doing the goose step on the bridle path in the middle of the Unter den Linden, was an unforgettable (and frightening) sight! If the informal and somewhat ragtag Red Army was to be the force to stop these monsters, then more power to them!

Much of my enthusiasm about the prospects for socialism in the

Soviet Union, about their factories, their farms, their enlightened prison system, their lifetime medical insurance, their guarantees of education, jobs and so forth had been transmitted to my parents in letters, which I asked them to retain in lieu of my writing the same material in the diary which I had been keeping since I was eleven. Here is an excerpt from one letter.

> I think Communism is the coming thing for the world. Don't be, like most Americans, shocked by this word. Don't think that there is any-thing horrible or violent about Communism. Unfortunately, the American press has seen fit to make people believe that the cause of all trouble in the U.S. lies with the so called "Reds," . . . with Commu-nists. I think a Communist state would mean more good for a greater number. The majority of people in America, as in all countries, are workers, but they get the fewest benefits from society.

My parents didn't need a siren to alert them to the fact that their pre-cious son was becoming very pro-Communist, and this was not exactly welcome news to conservative parental ears in 1934. The result was that both my mother and father came to New York to meet my boat, and although my father respected my intelligence enough not to attack my views head-on, he did turn me over to a lot of his mogul friends who could confront me harshly without undermining family relations.

A warning of things to come had been given me aboard the *SS Ma-jestic* on the westbound Atlantic crossing when I got a threatening cable from my mother. She knew ~~that~~ I had shaved my head and grown a beard in Moscow because I foolishly sent home some pic-tures. Some of my hair had grown back, but I still had a Lenin-style goatee and moustache, and my mother's edict was that if I got off the ship with the beard, she would leave the dock.

I resented the order to shave and had every intention of testing her determination to walk out, when I discussed the matter with the noted actor and columnist Will Rogers, who was traveling first class of course, and was also on his way back from the USSR. (I knew Rogers from Hollywood and had been a buddy of his son, Will Jr.—later a Congressman—during my two years at Stanford.) Rogers, by the way, was not as favorably impressed by the USSR as we were. But I liked him and respected him as a Roosevelt supporter and a decent human being who was on the right side of most social issues. (He had also invited Schulberg and me—traveling in third class—to join him for a meal in the posh first-class dining room.) When I told him the problem, he laughed and said my mother was doing me a favor with her order because, although he hated to say so, he thought I looked ridiculous with the "shrubbery" (as he called it). I then followed his advice and went to the ship's barber shop.

The seriousness of my defection from the movie mogul-mold becomes obvious if I list the names of the tycoons who took time out from their busy schedules to have at me and my pinko leanings. These meetings, arranged by my father with the best of intentions, began almost as soon as I landed, the first taking place in New York with two of the illustrious Warner brothers, to be followed on the West Coast during my Christmas vacation with Louis B. Mayer, David Selznick, and Irving Thalberg.

Abe Warner, who ran the East Coast activities of the family business, was the toughest of the lot. Known in the industry as "The Major" (for a reason that I never understood), he didn't want to discuss the issue with me. "You're a god-damned little fool," he said, "and you will cause a lot of trouble for all of us." His brother Harry, then president of the company, gave me the rueful bit: How could I do this to my father, who had done so much to see to it that I got the education he never had?

Louie Mayer, sitting beneath an autographed picture of dictator Benito Mussolini, told me that what I was doing was bad for the Jews because they were frequently identified with Communist causes. My turning Communist would strengthen the view that Jews and Communists were synonymous. Several books on Hollywood history by authors who interviewed me say that I answered him as only a fresh young punk could. Knowing that Mayer was featured in the press every year as "the highest paid corporate executive in the country," I am reported to have said, in answer to his charge that my being "red" was bad for the Jews, "I'll give up being a Communist if you'll give up being a capitalist." Let me set the record straight. I didn't say it; but it was the answer I thought of when I was leaving his office.

Selznick and Thalberg were younger men and—when I met with them separately—they treated me with more kindness and consideration than their older colleagues. Both said that they too had been radicals when they were twenty. They both considered this normal and desirable. Selznick said that he still read left-wing publications and he agreed with much of what he read, but he was primarily interested in making movies and couldn't serve two masters—politics and moviemaking. He preferred the movies and thought that if I wanted to make great movies some day, I would have to forget about politics and concentrate on learning the moviemaking process.

Thalberg invited me for lunch in the private dining room of his studio bungalow and also invited his associate and assistant, Albert (Allie) Lewin, a former professor and, according to Thalberg, an expert on Marxism, about which I knew very little at that time. The point of this was to have Lewin, the expert, punch holes in any Marxist theories I might advance. He did, and I had difficulty refuting him, but I maintained my favorable impression of the Soviet Union, based on what I had seen.

Let me conclude this chapter with another set of quotes from a Moscow letter:

> Right now I'm a little muddled as to what I'm going to do with my life. . . . I can't go into the picture business . . . and work into the big money and at the same time fight for Communism and be convinced that Communism is the right system for the world. I'd be playing a game with myself—living like a capitalist by day and like a Communist at night. . . . I will probably work in the picture business because I am fitted for that sort of work. . . . And since I intend to work for the greatest good for the greatest number, I should work at what I do best. But how I am going to approach this compromise I don't know yet. . . . You see, I don't fit anyplace in society as it is today. But I am going to have the whole of next year at school to figure it out.

Chapter 6

The Theater

It would have been very easy to go back to Hollywood after graduation and to start my career at the studio as a junior writer. But, having grown up with the studio as my playground, I graduated from college singularly lacking in awe of the movies. I believed ~~that~~ moviemaking was primarily a business and, while there was an occasional movie of genuine merit, the industry objectives—as carried out by the producers—were to attract audiences and to make money. As a dyed-in-the-wool leftie, I was convinced that if I wanted to do anything of lasting merit in the performing arts, I would have to work in what one still calls, with a touch of an English accent, "the theahtuh."

My father accepted my decision, no doubt thinking that I would spend a few years working on Broadway, get some experience studying live audiences, and would ultimately come back to the studio better equipped to turn out successful movies. So he used his influence with Sidney Phillips, the man in charge of MGM's New York theater department, to get me a job with a distinguished theatrical producer—Crosby Gaige. Unfortunately, the job paid only fifteen dollars a week, which, even in those days of breadlines and five-cent apples, would not buy many restaurant meals, would not pay the rent and, most important of all, would not buy tickets—even in the top balcony.

The solution was to moonlight. With my cousin Al Mannheimer, late of Yale and the trip to the USSR, and Steve Brooks, an unemployed business type who was in my graduating class at Dartmouth, we decided to launch a cultural news service that would be sold to small-town newspapers. We called it "Empire Features" and rented a one-room apartment at 30 Park Avenue because it gave us a fancy address to use on our stationery and a place for me to live. Mannheimer and I then contacted theatrical press agents in New York for review-ers' passes to plays, wrote to book publishers and record companies for review copies, and proceeded to write a weekly bulletin of gossip and play, book, and record reviews.

Believe it or not, we were soon on the second-night list for all the-atrical openings and continued to receive books and records for years to come. Brooks hit the road to visit the editors of small town papers in towns like White Plains, Poughkeepsie, Mount Kisco, and Tarrytown, offering "Empire Features" free for three weeks after which it could be continued for a nominal sum. With this arrangement, our material ap-peared for several weeks in at least six or seven weekly newspapers. We had high hopes for wide circulation, but when the time came to pay for a subscription to our service, all our subscribers canceled.

I did manage to double my own salary—an extra fifteen dollars a week—by selling reviews evaluating the movie potential of new plays as well as a Broadway gossip column to a Hollywood weekly pub-lished by a friend of mine who thought that the Rapf name (which he featured prominently) would lend respectability to his rag. After a couple of months it became obvious why he was willing to pay for this dubious respectability. *Hollywood Life,* the publication that fea-tured my writing and my byline, was a blackmailing scandal sheet and just before its publisher (my friend) was arrested, my father got wind of what was to happen and ordered me to pull my copy and give up my job.

As for eating, I got by four nights a week with a hot dog and an or-ange drink at Nedick's (fifteen cents) and got myself invited to rela-tives' apartments from time to time and to Sidney Phillips's house every Saturday night. Phillips became my mentor (as well as a source of good German food and drink and especially of spritzers—drinks concocted of white wine and soda) in New York. He worked for MGM, but I doubt that he ever went to the movies. He was strictly a man of the theater and an inveterate New Yorker, with his white shirts, bow ties, and tweed jackets. He had produced a few successful plays, was married to a mature actress named Mary Phillips, and in-evitably had people from the theater as Saturday night guests, in-cluding stage directors such as Worthington (Tony) Minor and his actress wife, Frances Fuller.

His job with the film company was ideal for him since MGM would, from time to time, back a Broadway production on the strength of Phillips's recommendation. They backed Sidney Kingsley's *Men in White*, for example, and had first call on the movie rights, which they exercised when they bought it and produced it. Thus, people sent Phillips their play scripts and he went to previews or openings almost every night in the week.

There were some 250 plays produced on Broadway in that season of 1935–1936 while I was working for Crosby Gaige. And some were very interesting: *Winterset, Idiot's Delight, First Lady, Boy Meets Girl, Porgy and Bess, Dead End, Victoria Regina,* among others. And there was also a flourishing left-wing theater in New York. Not just the midtown Group Theater, which became the showcase for the works of Clifford Odets, after *Waiting for Lefty,* and became the breeding ground for Hollywood actors such as John Garfield, Rod Steiger, Lee J. Cobb, and Frances Farmer. There was also the Theater Union in the Civic Repertory on 14th Street, the Theater of Action, the Artef Players, and others. Here, one could see the work of Brecht and of left-wing U.S. playwrights, actors, and directors such as Elia Kazan, Albert Maltz, George Sklar, Paul Peters, Victor Wolfson, and Michael Blankfort, most of whom I met.

One noteworthy play, introduced by the Theater Union at one of its Sunday night Civic Repertory performances and later moved uptown, was Irwin Shaw's *Bury the Dead,* a strong statement against war—as was Sidney Howard's adaptation of the Humphrey Cobb novel, *Paths of Glory* (later made into a stunning movie by Stanley Kubrick).

The years 1935 through 1936 were also the period of a thriving Federal Theater under the direction of Hallie Flanagan, formerly of Vassar College. The Federal Theater, which paid miserable wages, nevertheless gave employment to hundreds of theater folk, including Orson Welles and John Houseman, who produced their black *Macbeth* in Harlem during the 1935–1936 season.

If I say that the best creative minds are attracted to the movies today, this power to attract the best was certainly present in the theater in the mid-thirties. And the man I worked for—Crosby Gaige—was known to be one of the most tasteful and discriminating producers on Broadway. He had, after all, collaborated with the brilliant Jed Harris as the producer of *Broadway* and he was the producer of sophisticated plays by Benn W. Levy like *Accent On Youth.* Not only that, but I knew he had planned for the coming season a pair of Shakespearean plays (*Othello* and *Macbeth*), featuring the distinguished husband and wife acting team of Philip Merivale and Gladys Cooper, who, as he told me during our first interview, were to emulate the famed marital team of

Marlowe and Sothern when they took plays on the road after successful runs on Broadway. The plays were to be directed by the noted
Shakespearean scholar and director Henry Herbert.

It is true that my job was an ignominious one. I was Gaige's office
boy and worked under the aegis of his officious office manager and
secretary, Sylvia Greenfeld. I would have the privilege of reading
scripts that were submitted for production and would write comments. But my principal work was not of the brain but of the legs. I
took Gaige's weekly food column (he was a pre-TV Julia Child) across
town to the offices of the *World Telegram* and on other occasions took
the subway to Wall Street to the offices of Mr. Gaige's "angel," who
had the appropriate name of Mr. Gabriel. Subsequently, I learned
why the angel Gabriel was investing in Gaige's plays. He had a girlfriend who was given walk-on parts in the Merivale-Cooper *Macbeth*
and *Othello* and in a short-lived comedy, *Whatever Goes Up,* by Milton Lazarus, that followed.

What I discovered during my six months of apprenticeship in the
Gaige office was that Gaige had very little interest in the theater itself. He was a cultured gentleman, to be sure, with a handsome floor-
to-ceiling library in his 42nd Street office. He was interested in the
culinary arts, and there is no doubt that he wished for Merivale and
Cooper to knock the critics dead with their rendition of Shakespeare.
But he was paying himself a producer's fee whether a play succeeded
or failed. The only people taking a gamble were the investors, principally the angel, Gabriel.

Well, when his revivals of Shakespeare died and *Whatever Goes Up*
actually went "down," Gaige was by no means penniless, and it was
time for downsizing the office staff—namely the fifteen dollar a week
office boy. Me! I could stay on; he wanted me, he said, because he val-
ued my services (although he had disregarded my negative comments
on the Milton Lazarus comedy). The only hitch was that I would have
to work for nothing.

So that was the end of my career in the theater. My father was busy
preparing a film about a college reunion, an idea he got when he came
to my graduation and observed the bizarre shenanigans of alumni returning to the campus. When he got back to Hollywood, he in-
structed the story department to find him a story about a college reunion. They found one by George Oppenheimer and Finley Peter
Dunne Jr. (one son of the famed Irish humorist, the other being the
successful and liberal Philip Dunne at 20th Century–Fox). The stu-

dio bought the Oppenheimer-Dunne story and hired them to work on it. My father was dissatisfied with what they did. He held out the attractive bait of working on the project if I came back to California.

Convinced by this time that the lofty Broadway theater was as commercial as Hollywood, I did just that—and finally joined the Communist Party.

Chapter 7

Joining the CP

During my days in New York, I had read the *Daily Worker* and had gone to mass meetings, left-wing plays, and Russian movies at the Cameo. I usually took a lot of heat from my relatives but found support from mentor Sidney Phillips, who thought it unique that the son of a Hollywood producer should be so "red." But even though I was ripe for the plucking, no one in New York ever asked me to join the Communist Party.

As soon as I got back to Hollywood, however, someone who shall be nameless asked me to join a Marxist study group and I accepted eagerly, anxious to fortify myself with answers to the arguments that informed anti-Communists had been throwing at me. I attended the study group—surprised that I knew most of the others who were, in fact, employees at my father's studio. After about a month, the study leader—who came from what we in Hollywood always called "downtown"—suggested that I should join the Young Communist League. I did. I signed nothing. I simply started going to YCL meetings.

My YCL "cell" (that's what it was called) was a "downtown" group, though one member was a UCLA student and the daughter of a Los Angeles movie theater owner. Her boyfriend, also from UCLA, was the younger brother of a friend of mine from L.A. High. Our area of activity was to organize progressive youth activities in Los Angeles. I was assigned to work on a youth newspaper called *The Winner,* which usually featured athletic subjects on the front page and got around to politics inside. We put out a half dozen issues of this paper before I spoke to the Party rep and said that I thought I was out of place, since my work was in Hollywood, I was active in the writers' guild, and I had limited contacts downtown.

I was told that I was in the YCL to recruit friends in Hollywood who might be ripe for joining the YCL but not quite ready for the CP itself. As for me, I could attend Hollywood Communist Party meetings if I wanted and continue in the YCL at the same time. It was also suggested that I make a more active effort to recruit. Because my parents had a house at Malibu, it might be useful to organize beach parties to which I could invite young leftists—men and women—whom I knew.

An astute member of the Party said several years later that one of the reasons for the success of recruiting in Hollywood was the Party's reputation for attracting the prettiest women in town. And anyone attending those Malibu beach affairs would probably concur. Politics were discussed, to be sure, but, for the most part, it was sunning, swimming, playing volleyball and touch football, and, much of the time, just getting to know beautiful people.

The beach was certainly a fertile recruiting ground and those who were recruited soon found themselves in CP units that met weekly, discussed tactics in organizatons, discussed further recruiting, collected dues, sold literature, had sessions on current events, and usually included reports on some aspect of the writings of Marx, Engels, Lenin, or Stalin.

The Hollywood Communist Party was, ostensibly of necessity, a secret organization, but the personnel and location of the units changed frequently on orders from on high—which usually meant from "downtown." You only met the people in your own unit. The first group I recall was organized by age, an outgrowth of the fact that some of us were in the YCL. Then came geographical units, so that we got to know comrades in our immediate neighborhoods (which was extremely useful in political election years). Then we were organized along studio lines, getting to know representatives of other crafts who worked for the same employer—like musicians, readers, and publicists.

Later—and all this shuffling may have occurred in a different order—we were organized according to craft so we could have impact on our unions. Even when we were organized by neighborhood or studio, there were occasional meetings with fellow writers. These were called "fraction" meetings and often included nonparty members who were sympathetic with our objectives but, for reasons of their own, refused to make a formal Party commitment. Just what a "formal commitment" was, is hard to define. I was asked repeatedly in the fifties by agents of the HUAC or the FBI if I was a "card-carrying member." I would laugh and say I would never be stupid enough to carry a card indicating membership in the Communist Party. I may or may not have been on the Party rolls with a pseudonym, but, with a card or without, I considered myself a member of the Party until the day I stopped going to meetings—a step that was also taken without any formalities.

Once the United States got into the war as an ally of the Soviet Union, the Party was put in an anomalous position. It had to pledge its support to the war effort and to the no-strike pledge of organized labor. Revolutionary aims, such as they were, had to be put on the shelf, and the Party, which had entered its own candidate against FDR in every election in which I voted, put forth no candidate to run aginst FDR in 1944. The Party itself changed its name from Communist Party, U.S.A., to the Communist Political Association. Earl Browder, a very American-type Midwesterner (despite the fact that, with his moustache, he bore a faint resemblance to Hitler), remained as head of the new association and proclaimed Communism as "twentieth-century Americanism."

In some parts of the country, Party members came out of the closet and declared themselves, as Party members had done for many years in nonfascist European countries. The objective was to turn the "association" into a mass organization. Some of us in Hollywood urged that in order to gain acceptance, we come out of the closet, too. One of the reasons we were regarded with so much suspicion, we argued, was that we all led double lives, supporting progressive causes but denying our Party membership.

Whether bringing Communist affiliation into the open at this time would have warded off the vicious persecution that was to come after the war is a moot question, but the leaders voted down the proposal for openness, even though large meetings were held in the Hollywood area during the war, attended, at least in one case that I remember, by about three hundred people, some of whom were members of the Association, some of whom may have been fellow travelers and, most of whom I had never seen before and would never see again.

After the war, of course, the U.S. Communist Party's move toward a mass organization was sharply criticized by Communists abroad, notably by Jacques Duclos in France, who considered the U.S. movement "revisionist." So did the old guard leaders in this country, and Browder and his followers were soon purged.

To the best of my recollection, there had been no restriction on disagreement in the Party, but when a policy or action was adopted, support was expected. This method of encouraging debate with resulting unanimity was given the oxymoronic title of "democratic centralism."

I lived with this peculiar methodology for ten years. All of my best friends were members of the Party, and I saw them socially whether we were attending the same Party meetings or not. Although we were drawn together by a similarity of views and purpose, there were certain members who irritated the hell out of me, either because they were too pontifical, too orthodox, too longwinded, too chintzy (they wouldn't pay their dues), or even too sloppy. There were others I loved, only one of whom ever turned fink when the heat was on, and I must say that no one I really liked ever put the finger on me when testifying to save his or her own skin.

I never met anyone in the Party who advocated the violent overthrow of the government. There were quite a few—including me—who thought there might be a violent takeover by the extreme right, a fascist *putsch*. Some thought that the government had concentration camps ready to accommodate a roundup of "reds" in the event of open warfare with the Soviet Union. (I continued to believe in the existence of U.S. concentration camps long after I left the Party, and it wouldn't surprise me to learn that there are such camps ready to accommodate dissidents like me today.) There were also optimists with clouded crystal balls who consistently predicted there would be a revolution by labor (bloodless, of course) before another year had passed.

Let me explain now—as I never would before if asked by one of the inquisitors of the House Un-American Activities Committee—that I didn't leave the Party because of disaffection or disagreement with its policies. I had always disagreed with some of the policies, but I thought that the Party, on the whole, represented the best interests of the common people of the United States, men and women, blacks and whites, and, for the most part, supported the kinds of organizations in the political field, in civil rights, in unions, farms, ecology, and on the peace front that I would have supported even if I were not in the Party. I quit because I was tired of going to meetings. I was frankly bored with all the argument about tactics and had come around to a point of view that David Selznick had expressed to me more than ten years before: "You have to choose between politics and making movies."

Being involved with the Party (politics) took a lot of time. I went to meetings two or three times a week and wrote articles, speeches, and reports when I was not at meetings. I had too little time to pursue my craft as a screenwriter, and I was making little progress in my career.

As it turned out, I decided to leave Hollywood altogether because as long as I was there and available, I was called on with requests to do this or that in some kind of political organization. I was, for example, once asked to run for the Democratic County Committee and, with left support, got elected from the Westwood area where I lived. What it meant was another evening down the drain every week! I was just plumb tired of left-wing political activity. I would still read the *New Masses* and go to an occasional mass meeting and spout my leftist views wherever I went—but no more regular meetings. I had had it!

And then came the 1947 subpoenas! I heard that one subpoena had my name on it. I never found out whether that was true. But my father was still an executive at MGM, and I knew that if I was called before the committee it would be very embarrassing for him. I had been out of work for about two months since resigning from a job with Walt Disney (in 1947), and I told my father I wanted to go East to see if I could make a living as a freelance writer away from the movie industry. I also told him about the subpoenas and said that sooner or later, I would get into trouble because of my Communist reputation, so this seemed like a good time to make the break.

He was very reluctant to see me leave, especially with three grandchildren on whom he doted, but he thought that the "red scare" would soon blow over and I would be back. I thought so too. We were both wrong.

I will say this for my dear father. He was a self-made man who quite naturally disagreed with my socialist views. Alone, we argued quite vehemently. But when any one of his friends started to red-bait me—and they did quite often—he would come strongly to my defense. "I disagree with my son, but he's a good human being and his convictions are based on what he thinks will benefit mankind."

My brother Matthew, who stayed in Hollywood throughout the fifties and became very successful as the producer of TV shows such as *Loretta Young, Ben Casey,* and *Kojak,* was even more loyal to his renegade relative than my father was. He not only defended me openly but refused to hire anyone who had turned fink and "named names" during the red inquisition of the HUAC.

Bless them both. My family and I had a hard time for many years, but my father and brother were always behind us. Even in Hollywood, as will become evident in the next chapter.

Chapter 8

Working in Hollywood—The Unions

My adult working career in Hollywood began in April 1936. I was assigned to a small cubicle in the long barracks known as the "writers' building" on the MGM lot. (If you were well established, you might rate a couch and an easy chair. I had a desk, a typewriter and one extra wooden chair.) I had been in the office for about an hour, sharpening pencils, separating yellow paper from white, and using all the stalling tactics I could think of to put off reading the material that had already been written on the subject I was assigned to write. There was a knock on the door. I opened it and recognized at once the lady who had knocked. She wore a large hat and smoked a cigarette with a holder. She was Lillian Hellman, author of the 1934 Broadway play sensation *The Children's Hour.* I had no idea that she worked at MGM, but she revealed in a moment why she had knocked on the door of an insignificant junior writer:

"I wonder if you would like to join the Screen Writers Guild?"

Would I like to join the Screen Writers Guild? Would I like to eat, sleep, make love?

"Of course."

"You realize that the Guild is being attacked by the producers for proposing to tie up the sale of all literary material?" I told her that I didn't know much about any of the Guild problems, that I had just arrived in town, but that I supported workers against employers in any event. (She undoubtedly knew my name, that I was considered a rebel despite being the son of an MGM executive.) She was careful to point out that her visit was taking place during her lunch hour and then gave me a form to sign and I was a member of the Screen Writers Guild.

I have already explained that the invasion of new personnel from the East, brought about by the new technological needs required for shooting sound, accelerated the move toward unionization and social awareness. It did not, however, mark the beginning of unions in the movie industry. One branch of the movie industry was unionized from the very start—the projectionists.

It came about like this. When the popularity of the movie medium convinced some entrepreneurs that real theaters, rather than con- verted shoe stores, were needed to satisfy audiences, the first moves were made to legitimate theaters (those used for stage plays) and vaudeville houses. History tells us that Koster and Bial's Music Hall was the first theater to run movies along with its stage shows in 1896. Big city theaters had been under the jurisdiction of an AF of L union, the International Alliance of Theatrical Stage Employees, familiarly known since 1893 by its acronym, IATSE. Stagehands belonged to this union so it was logical that the new theater employees—the pro- jectionists—should be forced to join. The first projectionists' local was established in 1906.

The IATSE hold on the projectionists ultimately became nation- wide and gave the union a loaded revolver to point at the heads of the big theater-studio chains: deal with us or we pull the projectionists. (No one needed a diagram to know that if the projectionists were "pulled," the movie business would come to a halt.) The craft unions—carpen- ters, painters, and electricians—had operated in Hollywood during the twenties without having a serious conflict with management. Same with the studio stagehands, who were members of IATSE.

Labor trouble came with the advent of sound, when the IA and the rival electricians' union each claimed jurisdiction over the new Hol- lywood sound technicians. There was an industry-wide strike in 1930, in which goons from the Teamsters were used to strong arm opponents of the IA. (My recollection of this strike is based on a tragic incident: The husband of my father's secretary, Mildred Kelley, on strike against his will, committed suicide.)

Most studios signed with the IA, but Columbia would not. In- dustry electrical workers and carpenters supplied replacements for IA people on strike at Columbia. Some IA people joined the craft unions so they could go back to work. It was the beginning of an industry- wide split among the crafts, known as "back lot" workers, that would go on into the postwar period and would lay the groundwork for charges and countercharges that would make a "red-scare" in the in- dustry possible.

It is important to recognize that the thirties saw the birth of a new union movement to challenge the entrenched craft unions in the AFL, which had, in some ways, become elitist and turned its backs on organizing the unorganized. That role fell to a new amalgam, the Council of Industrial Organization, known as the CIO, which sought to organize the unorganized in the auto industry and in steel and to organize on an industry, rather than a craft basis.

The IATSE, although part of the AFL, was made up of several craft unions, and it began to envision the possibility of organizing studio workers on an industry-wide basis. The IATSE took its first steps in 1935, using the familiar but effective threat of a projectionists' strike to force all of the major studios to recognize its jurisdiction. (The IA was then under the leadership of George Browne and Willie Bioff, who had connections to Chicago gangsters, and it was later revealed that they accepted a payoff from the studios to keep their union in line after signing. One producer, Joseph M. Schenck of 20th Century–Fox, was chosen as the "fall guy" by the producers and served a jail sentence for his part in the bribe. Browne and Bioff ultimately lost their posts in the union and leadership went to Roy Brewer, who became a leading figure in the purge of so-called "reds" after the war.)

Some of the crafts people—notably the painters and carpenters—were not part of the contract signed in 1935 with the IA. They set up a rival group, the Federated Motion Picture Crafts, which would eventually evolve into the Conference of Studio Unions under Herb Sorrell of the painters' union, who was then considered to be a radical. The CSU was unique, in that it was joined by organizations of white collar workers like the publicists, the readers, and the set designers. Studio management could see the incubation of industrial unionism in the CSU and feared, with some justification, an imminent invasion by the CIO.

Meanwhile, the heady prospect of union organization was infecting the three major areas of talent—the actors, the directors, and the writers. Part of this was due to the arrival of new, union conscious talent from the East; part was the result of some arbitrary, dictatorial actions by the previously benevolent and paternal employers—these being the unnecessary 50 percent salary cut and the coercion to support Republican Merriam in his campaign for governor against the liberal Upton Sinclair.

Each talent group had organized a "guild," as befit its cultural status, rather than a "union," which might have implied that members were working class, which, as employees, they certainly were. In any case, representatives of the three groups met and formed an "Inter-Talent Council," presumably with the intention of acting in concert to achieve recognition by the studios.

The actors seemed to be the most militant of the three groups. Although leading actors were well paid, there was an army of thousands of extras and bit players who earned very little when they worked. As far as I know, none of these poverty-level performers was on the board of the Screen Actors Guild, but they showed up for mass meetings at the Hollywood Legion Stadium (scene of weekly prizefights on Wednesday nights) to hear President Robert Montgomery and militant actors like Ronald Reagan rabble-rouse against the studios on their behalf.

In the end—1935, to be exact—the actors decided to abandon the directors and writers to get their own contract. They joined the AFL and, with the clout of that national organization—already playing footsie with the producers through the IATSE—the actors got their contract. That was the end of the Inter-Talent Council.

Which brings us back to one of the most interesting labor struggles in movie history—and one that began for me when Lillian Hellman signed me up as a member; it was the formation, dissolution, and ultimate recognition of the Screen Writers Guild, now known as the Writers Guild of America.

The day Hellman signed me up, she invited me to a meeting that night at the home of Samson Raphaelson, another name that was familiar to me because of his work in both theater and film, and I assured her I would be there. It was one of many meetings I attended during the next week. I got the drift of the discussions—the problems that had to be met—but, most of all, I sat in awe of the people in attendance: Hellman and her friend Dashiell Hammett, Edwin Justus Mayer, Donald Ogden Stewart, Samuel Hoffenstein, Dorothy Parker and Alan Campbell, Ogden Nash, S. J. Perelman, and the movie names I knew such as Ernest Pascal, Sonya Levien, Sam Hellman, and Dudley Nichols. What was I—a twenty-two-year-old novice—doing in the company of these literary celebrities? I probably would have supported their program even if it meant blowing up a studio or two.

But it did not. This group simply wanted to be recognized by the producers as the legitimate representative of screenwriters, with details of the contract to be worked out later. It was clear that they sought increased control of their written material, including the right to decide credits and improvements in working conditions, notably having to do with speculative writing and ending the odious practice of having more than one writer assigned to a project without any one of them being informed. There were actually no economic demands, although later there would be argument within the Guild as to the desirability of a minimum wage (since my first salary was forty dollars a week, I was very happy when a one-hundred-dollar minimum was agreed upon).

The producer's association had refused all requests to negotiate. The Guild, already loosely affiliated with the New York–based Authors Guild and Dramatists Guild, then sought a more formal connection to form a national writers' organization that would impose a boycott on the sale of all literary material to the studios or the signing of any contracts extending beyond May 2, 1938.

To put the boycott into effect, the Guild would amalgamate with the Authors Guild and the Dramatists Guild as part of the Authors League. And it was this step—the formal amalgamation with Eastern writers' organizations—that became the nominal bone of contention among West Coast writers, a contention largely fomented by the studios themselves. What the studios really opposed was organization itself; what they did was spread the word that amalgamation meant surrendering control of the industry to an unsavory bunch of Eastern writers who were "reds." And since there were a fair number of prominent writers who supported the studio position—some who were so conservative that they refused to think of themselves as union members at all, some who were so well paid that they didn't want to risk upsetting the apple cart—it stood to reason that when the amalgamation would come to a vote on May 2, 1936, there would be stiff opposition.

What happened instead was a love-fest. There had been a high-level meeting before the general meeting, in which the opponents of amalgamation made their case. They favored a Guild contract, or so they said, but they wanted to clean up some of the ambiguities in the proposed agreement with the Eastern writers' guilds. It was agreed, therefore, that the amalgamation would be voted in principal, that representatives of the opposition would be appointed to the Guild Board, and that there would be another meeting for approval after changes were made in about a month.

It was a genuine armistice that seemed to please everyone. Dorothy Parker, a member of the outgoing board that had favored amalgamation, actually embraced James Kevin McGuinness, who had led the opposition. She had tears of joy in her eyes. We all cheered the result and many of us repaired to the Hollywood Athletic Club bar to drink ourselves silly because of what we deemed an unexpected victory.

The celebration was short-lived. My recollection is that some of the opposition faction who had been appointed to the Guild board resigned within a day or two. Shortly thereafter the *Hollywood Reporter* announced that the Producers Association had recognized a new writers' organization, the Screen Playwrights, one of whose chief officers was the very same McGuinness and most of whose members were the very same people who had opposed amalgamation in the Guild. The producers gave the new organization a contract.

The Screen Writers Guild, as it had been constituted, was in shambles. President Ernest Pascal may have abdicated, for all I knew. Most members resigned. I did not, though there was actually no organization left. In the months that followed, there were rumors that some of the staunchest former Guild supporters (Allen Rivken was one) were being blacklisted (denied employment). The Screen Playwrights, with their contract, attracted a few new members. The old Guild was moribund.

My memory is very fuzzy about what happened in that year of inaction, but one incident stands out as proof that there had indeed been a deal between the producers and the leaders of the Screen Playwrights. My collaborator, Dick Maibaum, and I had an office next to James McGuinness in a one-story building near the Motor Avenue gate at MGM. Late one afternoon we heard the muffled sounds of yelling from McGuinness's office. By putting my ear to a drinking glass pressed to the wall, it was possible to make out what the ruckus was about. McGuinness liked to drink, so it was not unusual for him to launch into verbal fireworks. This time the content of his outburst was extraordinary and justified my sharing the listening glass with Maibaum. The gist of it was repeated over and over again: "I'll show that Jew bastard that loyalty is not a one-way street." There were mumbles from whomever his listener was, then more from Jim, "God damn it, loyalty is not a one-way street."

The listener, as we discovered by leaving our door ajar to see him when he left, was Harry Edington, McGuinness's agent. The cause of the outburst was revealed when word got around that Irving Thalberg had removed McGuinness as the producer of a movie called *Maytime* after ostensibly having promised to make him a producer in return for his role in breaking up the SWG. So the "Jew bastard" was Thalberg, and the "loyalty" was McGuinness's commitment to the studio position, a "one-way street" since it had gone unrewarded.

The Guild was reactivated in 1937 when it was learned ~~that~~ we could seek recognition as industry employees by the National Labor Relations Board (NLRB) and then could hold an industry-wide election to determine which organization—SWG or Screen Playwrights or none at all—should represent employed writers in labor negotiations. Once a bargaining agent was certified, the employers could be compelled to negotiate.

The prospect of using the NLRB to gain recognition for writers raised some troublesome questions having to do with art versus industry. Were screenwriters really workers? A lot of staunch SWG members did not think so. There was a big difference between a screenwriter and a steelworker or a guy on an assembly line. On the other hand, the movie writer worked for a weekly paycheck; in many studios, he was checked in and out at the gate as if he were punching a time clock. His output was owned lock, stock, and barrel by his employer, who was described in contracts as "the author," and the boss could fire him without notice.

The vast majority of writers thought ~~that~~ their working conditions could be improved and saw the Guild as a useful medium through which to deal collectively with the producers. We were confident, therefore, ~~that~~ we could win the NLRB-sponsored election. And we did, though not without a vigorous organizing effort at every studio since the vote was to be conducted at each studio rather than being industry-wide.

Winning the election by no means guaranteed a contract with the producers. It was at least two years before a Minimum Basic Agreement was reached between the Guild and the Producers' Association. And, although I was a relative novice with only a few screen credits, I was a member of the negotiating committee. Let me, with full candor, explain why:

I was a member of the Communist Party and there was, frankly, sufficient left-wing influence in the Guild to elect any Communist-sponsored slate. So I was elected to the board four times between 1938 and 1946, serving twice as secretary. My particular interest and expertise was the Guild's credit system, and I became chairman of the Credit Arbitration Committee in 1939. It was in this capacity that I wrote the first set of rules for Guild arbiters and worked out the basis for our credit demands in the proposed contract with the producers.

That was one of the reasons I served on the negotiating committee. The other was less savory. I had a special notoriety as the left-wing son of a producer at a major studio. For me to participate in contract negotiations with the producers' committee, most of them close associates of my father who had known me since childhood, was as embarrassing to me as it was to them. My father actually warned me against being "used" by my Guild colleagues in this way.

There was one meeting—in a private dining room behind the Hollywood Brown Derby on Vine Street—when I was called upon to explain the credit demands in our proposed contract. These demands were really quite simple. The studios would have the right to issue tentative credits on any film about to be released. A notice would be sent to all writers who had been employed on a given project. These writers would have four days to object tentatively to the producers' designation and to request that they have access to the written material on which the producers' credits were based. This meant, essentially, seeing the final screenplay to determine whether one's contribution was sufficient to justify credit or not. (The rule of thumb at that time was that a single writer should have contributed 25 percent of the final screenplay in order to receive screenplay credit, and a team would be required to contribute a third.)

If a writer, after reading the material, still objected to the studio's designation, he would meet with other writers to see if agreement could be reached. If not, the project would go to Guild arbitration and a committee of three would be appointed, usually three people working at a given studio, to read the material and make a binding decision. In this way, the final control of credits—which we recognized as the principal factor that determined pay scales—was, after the studio's initial designation, entirely under the control of the writers. (I should mention that the arbitration committees based their decisions on written work, not on oral testimony. The most troublesome case I recall was that of *Hangmen Also Die* when Berthold Brecht, who spoke no English, was represented by the composer Hans Eisler and lost out to John Wexley who had put his own name on every page of the script which Eisler insisted had been written in collaboration by the two writers speaking to each other in German.)

In describing the Guild's procedure to the producers' committee— and it was ultimately accepted as part of the contract—I happened to say at one point, "In the past, producers violated equitable procedure by failing to notify *all* the writers." This caused the MGM representative on the bargaining committee, Eddie Mannix, to stand up in indignation and say, "I am not going to sit here and listen to this snot nose tell us that we violate anything." And he stormed out of the room. For a moment, there was stunned silence. The producers' chairman, Y. Frank Freeman of Paramount, said, "I suggest ~~that~~ we proceed." The Guild committee should have walked out at that point, to support me as one of its members. They did not, but I did not speak again. We went on to another subject. My father was right. I was being used and did not get the support I deserved.

One of the most bitterly fought strikes in the industry occurred early in 1941 at Walt Disney's studio. This was especially ironic because Disney, his studio, and his films had been widely praised by the intellectual liberal elite, and his refusal to negotiate with the fledgling Screen Cartoonists Guild came as an unwelcome shock, which, in later years, many who knew Disney well attributed to bad advice.

In any case, Disney had a very paternal relationship with his employees, and, like many other bosses who sought to avert genuine labor organization, he encouraged the establishment of a company union. But after the success of *Snow White* (released in 1937) and his move to a new and elaborate studio in Burbank, his next two features—*Pinocchio* and *Fantasia*—were financial flops. Working conditions at Disney were probably better than at other animation studios, but there were lay-offs. And when Walt made the mistake of firing one of his most gifted animators, Art Babbitt, who had resigned from the Disney company union to join the Screen Cartoonists' Guild, the action precipitated a strike which lasted nine weeks and resulted in a victory for the Cartoonists' Guild.

When I went to work at Disney's as World War II was drawing to a close, the strike was just a memory but not a very pleasant one. Among my good friends were those who had struck as well as those who had remained faithful to Walt. But one thing was clear. Even the faithful were less than enthusiastic about their patron's paternalism. They didn't like the sale of Disney artifacts such as comic books, stuffed ducks, and Mickey Mouse watches near the cash register in the studio commissary, and few had any confidence in the future of Disney common stock. How wrong they were! And how would they have felt about Disneyland?

It is important to bear in mind that studio labor struggles were being waged against a background of international turbulence and that Hollywood personnel were being drawn ever more prominently into the forefront of domestic and international issues. The growth of the Communist Party in Hollywood had a lot to do with this. The studios, who had their informers and labor spies, knew this, and ultra-conservative members of the community—many of whom were members of the Screen Playwrights—did their best to promote a "red scare." Disney, for example, was convinced that the Guild strike against his studio was fomented by a left-wing group in the AFL led by the head of the painter's union, Herb Sorrell.

People often assume that the "red scare" and the industry blacklist that followed the 1947 hearings of the House Un-American Activities Committee were strictly postwar phenomena. They were not. The conflict had its roots in the thirties with the growth of unionism, with Upton Sinclair's Epic movement (which stood for End Poverty in California), with the organized boycott of Japanese goods (including silk stockings) after that country invaded Manchuria. It also had roots in the formation of an Anti-Nazi League, the support for the Loyalists in the Spanish Civil War, the campaign for collective security in the League Against War and Fascism, and, last but not least, the campaign to help the migrant farm workers in California (the Steinbeck Committee to Aid Agricultural Organization).

I will devote an entire chapter to the movie industry blacklist, but it is important to remember that Martin Dies, the first chairman of the HUAC, brought his committee to Hollywood in 1939, that a musician turned legislator named Jack Tenney (composer of *Mexicali Rose*) headed a California state investigation committee, and that the disgruntled leaders of the defunct Screen Playwrights joined with others of similar political views in an organization known as the Motion Picture Alliance for the Preservation of American Ideals. Rumor has it that this organization actually urged HUAC to launch its hearings in 1947. Whether true or not, the Alliance members certainly used the "red scare" to justify the inquisition that will be described in a later chapter.

To finish the union story, I must mention the last violent movie industry strike. It took place at Warner Bros. in 1945 but it was ill-timed because it violated labor's wartime no-strike pledge. Then—with the help of red-baiting, the Los Angeles police department, and a few machine guns well-placed on the roofs of studio buildings by studio manager Blaney Matthews—Roy Brewer of the IATSE took on and defeated Herb Sorrell's Conference of Studio Unions, to end, once and for all, the threat of industrial unionism in the industry. Since the remnants of the left wing in the other unions tried desperately but without success to rally support for the CSU strikers, the defeat laid the groundwork for successful attacks on anyone suspected of left-wing leanings one year later.

Party members on the board of the Screen Writers Guild went out on a shaky limb to urge support of Sorrel's striking unionists. Some of us showed up at Warners' to march on the picket lines. But we were pushing our writer colleagues too far, and when the strike was lost we who had urged support lost face.

The closest thing we ever had to unity in the Hollywood labor movement came about in the fifties, when the unions fell in line behind the studios in demanding that their members sign loyalty oaths in order to work or, in the SWG, to get screen credit (something the Writers Guild, West, has atoned for recently in trying to restore lost credits).

Now, what was it like to work as a screenwriter in the old Hollywood?

Chapter 9

Writing for the Screen

As the reader can surmise from the detailed information in the previous chapter, I was probably more deeply involved in union activities than in pursuing my career as a writer of movies. For one thing, my writing career did not start too auspiciously. When my father urged me to quit the theater and come west, I was employed as a junior writer and earned forty dollars a week. My first collaborator, Dick Maibaum, an ex-University of Iowa drama instructor, had had a play produced on Broadway and had a seven-year contract that began at $200 a week and could be renewed or dropped every six months.

We worked for my father on the college reunion story called *We Went to College*. Maibaum and I were familiar with the foibles of college dramatics, and we made our hero a former college actor who had been romantically involved with a local actress, whom he abandoned after commencement. She subsequently married one of the hero's classmates, who stayed in the college town and became a professor. The hero's return to the campus for his twentieth reunion rekindles the old romance—at least as far as the former sweetheart is concerned—and causes complications for many, especially the hero's wife. Our script was well-liked, and for a short time it was touted as a vehicle for William Powell and Myrna Loy, who were at the peak of their popularity as Nora and Nick Charles in the *Thin Man* series.

Unfortunately, Maibaum and I were novice writers and no director of importance (my father tried to interest Victor Fleming) was willing to take a chance on a script written by unknowns. So when our script was shot, it was with lesser-known actors and with an imported journeyman director named Joseph Santley. Walter Abel and Edith Atwater were cast in the Powell-Loy parts and the rest of the

103

cast was filled with comedians—Hugh Herbert, Charley Butterworth, Walter Catlett, Una Merkel—all excellent performers but not exactly marquee names. It was intended to be a comedy and was played as such. There was a successful preview in the working-class neighborhood of Huntington Park. The studio brass thought they had a comedy sleeper on their hands.

The day after the preview, studio manager Eddie Mannix called me into his office to congratulate me. He then asked what my salary was. When I told him it was $40 a week, he realized I had been paid the princely sum of $480 for twelve weeks' work on the movie. He offered me a bonus of $500. I said I would much prefer to have a raise to $75 a week, but he refused to give it to me so I took the bonus.

I suppose I was lucky to get anything. There was a second preview—for the trade paper critics—a week or so later at the Ritz Theater on Wilshire Boulevard, where the clientele is drawn from the surrounding Jewish neighborhood. The preview was booked for the same night as a scheduled Joe Louis–Max Schmeling boxing match (they were the leading contenders for a crack at champion James J. Braddock); important fights were always broadcast on the radio, and since Pacific Time is three hours behind Eastern Standard, the fight would start at six. In this case, the fight was over by 7:30 because Schmeling (a German and an avowed Nazi, who would later be congratulated by Hitler) knocked out the "Brown Bomber" in the twelfth round—Joe Louis's only defeat up to that time. It was a sad night for the whole country and especially for Jews.

The preview went on at 8:30 and what had been a hilarious comedy in Huntington Park didn't get a single laugh in the Ritz theater after the Schmeling knockout of Joe Louis. We knew the movie had bombed, and the next day when I picked up *The Hollywood Reporter* near the studio entrance, I saw the headline above the third page review: it read, *"We Went to College Dull."* I kept the paper, but I didn't go into the studio. I went home.

There is a happy ending to the story, however. A month or so later, *We Went to College* played the Capitol Theater in New York. Frank Nugent, the *New York Times* film critic and later the successful writer of most of the fifties' John Ford westerns (he had become Ford's son-in-law), said of *We Went to College* that it was "about as pleasant a comedy as we have seen this year." Then he went on to say, "It is no less a credit to the MGM studio than *The Great Ziegfeld, San Francisco,* and some of the other more opulent movies which cost more to produce, will earn more at the box office but, on a pro rata basis, are no richer in entertainment." Naturally, Dick Maibaum and I regarded Nugent as the most astute movie critic in the nation.

Darryl Zanuck, production chief at 20th Century–Fox, had, as I later learned, quite a different opinion because the *Times'*s reviewer seemed to lambast all Fox pictures, especially the highly popular movies with Tyrone Power and Alice Faye. Zanuck, a notorious practical joker, decided to get even with Nugent for his critical abuse of Fox pictures. Sometime around 1940, he offered Nugent a lucrative contract, brought him to the Fox studio as a script doctor, gave him a series of assignments to "fix" scripts by others, and summarily rejected everything that Nugent wrote or suggested. After a few years, Nugent was demoralized and his contract wasn't renewed. But by this time, he had rented a house in the L.A. area, he had been replaced on the *Times,* and he had to face the future as an unemployed screenwriter.

The Nugent story, like that of *We Went to College,* has a happy ending because, after the war, Nugent started writing for John Ford, and one can see his name on *Fort Apache, She Wore a Yellow Ribbon, The Quiet Man, The Searchers,* and other Ford classics. And in the late fifties Nugent was elected president of the Screen Writers Guild.

The persecution of Nugent wasn't the only example of sadism indulged in by the otherwise estimable and brilliant Mr. Zanuck. He hired the ex-flyweight champion, Fidel La Barba—a graduate of Stanford—as a screenwriter but used him primarily as a sparring partner in the studio gym. La Barba could have flattened his boss in one of their boxing sessions but he obviously held his punches. Until it was too late. Zanuck, with the smirky knowledge of his circle of stooges, gave La Barba something to drink that caused him to pee green, scared the hell out of him, and then fired him.

It must be admitted, however, that, as head of production at Fox, Zanuck had a remarkably successful record. He was known for his ability to "save" scripts in trouble and, following previews, to recut finished films with a magic touch. Not everyone was enamored of the Zanuck touch, though. It was said that John Ford had such a clear idea of what *My Darling Clementine* should look like that he shot it with a minimum of camera angles and said, as he turned the footage over to Zanuck's favorite editor, Barbara McLean, "Let's see what the son of a bitch can do to change that."

One of my script experiences with Zanuck after I left MGM was equally upsetting. Fox was shooting a comedy with John Barrymore, a notorious drunk, playing himself as *The Great Lover.* Cast and crew and editors were in stitches as the film progressed, and Zanuck was eager to do an immediate sequel. I was assigned to write it from a story devised by the producer, Milton Sperling. It was based on a real-life character: a famous radio personality known as "Uncle Don," who was adored by children to whom he read stories but who was actually a drunk and whoremonger. (He was called "Uncle Whoa Bill" in my script.)

It seems that after one program, when the engineer failed to turn off Uncle Don's mike, he finished his saccharine spiel to the kiddies and, thinking the mike was off, added, "Well, that ought to hold the little bastards." That message went out on the air waves and marked finis to the career of lovable Uncle Don and my fictional "Uncle Whoa Bill."

This was a perfect part for the charming drunk and roué John Barrymore, except that I finished the script at about the same time *The Great Lover* was previewed. The comedy that had had everyone at the studio in stitches now laid a big egg. My script for Barrymore was headed for the ashcan when Sperling and I were summoned to Zanuck's office.

Zanuck usually came to the studio around noon; he was the only person allowed to park a car on the studio side of the administration building so that everyone would know when he was in his office. The car, after all, was unique—a Cadillac phaeton (convertible touring car) in Zanuck green, a color that graced his offices, his steam room, and all the Zanuck automobiles. Zanuck himself frequently wore a polo player's outfit with jaunty jodhpurs and carried a polo mallet as if he had just left the field. He would pace up and down his office with a big cigar in his mouth, talking a blue streak and swinging the mallet, but careful not to hit any of his hunting trophies—such as a lacquered elephant's hoof that was used as a coffee table.

On this occasion he gave his reasons (which we already knew) for canceling our project, but then said that the idea was too good to throw away and ~~that~~ he had come up with the solution for saving it. Instead of John Barrymore, we would use Guy Kibbee as Uncle Whoa Bill. I was in the hot seat—a stiff-backed chair reserved for writers across from Zanuck's throne behind the desk. "But Kibbee is a lovable old man whom no one would believe capable of drinking or chasing women," I said. "And he would never say, 'That ought to hold the little bastards.'" Zanuck nodded. He didn't claim the switch would be easy. But it could be accomplished. And he proceeded to outline the entire film, with a lovable old man rather than a lascivious drunk as the idol of a million kids.

Sperling and I left the office in a daze. Our project was "alive," but neither of us thought Zanuck's notion had made it "well." And we were more convinced than ever of the impossibility of the switch when—on the following day—we received Dorothy Hechtlinger's eighteen-page transcription of Zanuck's words of wisdom. Besides, there was an addendum: "This could be a definitive picture of big-time radio so I strongly suggest hiring an experienced radio writer to work with Rapf on the rewrite." Sperling obeyed. I should have resigned from the project. Instead, I tried to collaborate with the "experienced radio writer" for several weeks. But Zanuck's idea was hopeless and I quit two weeks before the new draft was completed and learned later that Zanuck had shelved the entire project.

Looking back on those years of struggling for recognition, I realize that I wasn't very good at my craft. I came to the industry with a certain innate ability, but I didn't improve. Part of the trouble was the amount of time spent on left-wing activities, part was a certain lack of awe and respect for the medium itself, and part was just an absence of luck.

When I left MGM and the sinecure of working for my father, the question wasn't asked outright by would-be employers, but it must have occurred to them to wonder, "Why should I hire him when he could be working for his father?" I remember one of my first interviews after leaving MGM. It was with Pandro Berman, then the head of production at RKO and a good friend of my family. "Why," he asked, "do you want to work for me?" "Because," I said, "I am interested in writing movies that have an important social message to deliver and I would consider it an honor and a privilege to work for a man who produced a film like *Winterset.*" (This movie, based on the prize play by Maxwell Anderson, was about the son of an anarchist like Sacco or Vanzetti seeking retribution from the judge who sentenced his father to death for a crime he did not commit.)

Berman gave me an icy stare. "*WINTERSET*! I should never have made it and won't ever make anything like it again." I was puzzled. "Why not?" "Because as head of production I am responsible to the stockholders, and I made that movie to please myself—not to make money." Needless to say, my enthusiasm for the social content of *Winterset* didn't get me the job.

I once told the plot of a story to Katharine Hepburn for whom the story had been written. It was called *Blaze of Glory* and was about a woman aviator modeled very specifically on a male aviation hero, Charles Lindbergh. The male lead in the story—to be played by Spencer Tracy—was modeled on Jimmy Doolittle, who bombed Tokyo. During the twenties, the Tracy character and the heroine had been lovers. Then the heroine flies the Atlantic solo, becomes famous, marries the son of a prominent and wealthy man, suffers the loss of a child through kidnapping, and falls from favor when she opposes support for Britain in World War II. It was the Lindbergh story transposed for Hepburn. Her old flame, Doolittle (to be played by Spencer Tracy), becomes a hero (bombing Tokyo) when she becomes persona non grata.

I thought it was a good story and perfect for Hepburn and Tracy (since they had, at the time, a real-life relationship). She liked it too, but said she wouldn't do it. "The world has too few heroes," she said. "I don't want to debunk one."

This business of writing original stories and trying to sell them when you are unemployed is not generally understood for what it is by students of the movies. An unemployed writer who writes originals for sale is essentially working for the industry without pay. When I worked in Hollywood, there were approximately five hundred employed writers and another thousand looking for work—most of them writing originals that could be described as screen stories written on speculation because they had no value unless they were bought or produced. One insidious practice that has largely been eliminated by stringent Guild rules has to do with "picking writers' brains" without compensation. It used to work this way: a producer has a story or script that he thinks is in need of work. He gives it to a series of unemployed writers who read it and make suggestions. The producer is under no obligation to hire anyone but he gets a lot of free advice.

There is another foible in the screenwriting lexicon that can be put into practice whether a writer is employed or not. This has to do with a singular method of plotting that was taught to me by a producer who became famous as the "Keeper of the B's." His name was Bryan Foy, and he was one of the children of a famous turn of the century vaudevillian, Eddie Foy, whose act was immortalized in a 1955 movie with Bob Hope called *The Seven Little Foys*.

Foy used to boast about the fact that he had taken the plot of one movie and made it a dozen times. The original, he said, was *Tiger Shark*, which featured Eddie Robinson as the middle-aged captain of a fishing boat who has the misfortune to lose his hand to a hungry shark. Robinson is married to a youngish woman (Zita Johann) who falls in love with his mate and best friend (Richard Arlen). He soon suspects some hanky-panky between the younger people and plans some skulduggery of his own to get revenge.

Well, Foy's attitude was that if it worked once, it could work again. All he and his writers had to do was to change the background. I no longer remember all of his adaptations, but I do remember a couple: one in a circus (lion tamer loses his hand to one of his beasts) and one in a lumber camp where the culprit was the buzz saw. And if the background wasn't suitable for the loss of a limb, there was always blindness, disfigurement, or an incurable disease.

I wasn't given this sure-fire plot formula in the abstract. I was working for Foy at the time. My assignment was to adapt a biography of a famous war correspondent, Floyd Gibbons, whose claim to fame was that he was always willing to risk his life to get a story. He was a news daredevil, who was said to have lost an eye on the field of battle while going across no-man's land with the troops. He always wore an eye-patch. The trouble was, he was a nut.

Foy said there must be some other stories about "nuts" who succeed because they are willing to risk their lives. I mentioned a recent MGM movie called *Test Pilot,* which featured Clark Gable as a daredevil aviator whose wife fears for his life every time he tests a plane. Foy's eyes lit up. He sent for a print, we looked at it and he said, "Perfect. It's an MGM picture; you should be able to get the script." Since my father was an important producer at MGM, I knew I could. But why?

"Because what I want you to do is follow the script scene by scene, line by line, except switch the background from aviation to journalism and radio broadcasting (Gibbons did radio shows.) Switch the hero from a test pilot to a reporter. It will work. He is on his way to a big story, his car has a flat tire on a road in front of a farm. He meets a girl who gives him a hard time but he takes her to a ball game—just like in *Test Pilot*—only change it to a carnival. And they fall in love, they marry, and she leaves with him without knowing what she is getting into." (In *Test Pilot*, Gable's plane crashes in Kansas and he meets Myrna Loy, whose family owns the farm land where the plane crashes. Gable falls for Loy and takes her away with him after a whirlwind courtship.)

I couldn't believe what I was hearing. I pointed out that this was plagiarism, and that's when he told me about the twelve versions of *Tiger Shark.* I pointed out that when he did all those versions of *Tiger*

Shark for Warner Bros., he was at least stealing from a Warner Bros. movie. I even reminded him that *Tiger Shark* itself may have been derived from the Warner Bros. version of *Moby Dick* which that studio made with John Barrymore in the twenties. After all, Captain Ahab's bitterness comes from having lost a leg to a whale early on. But *Test Pilot* belonged to MGM and we were now at 20th Century–Fox. Needless to say, I didn't last on that assignment and it pleases me to add that the Floyd Gibbons story was never made.

Foy's technique is sometimes called in respectable terms "using a template." And he wasn't the only one to acknowledge—even to boast about—use of the "template" method. A producing team at Paramount, William Pine and William Thomas, sometimes known as the "Dollar Bills" because they were so good at turning out cheap movies, boasted that they based almost all their movies on an old play by "Spig" Wead called *Ceiling Zero,* which was actually made into a good movie by Warner Bros. in 1935. It had an easily switchable plot—originally about a brash young mail pilot (played by Jimmy Cagney) who gives his more conservative boss and friend (Pat O'Brien) grey hairs when he breaks all the rules and goes on the make for a young female flyer. One of his friends dies in a crash and Cagney is regenerated, so, as I said, it is easily transposable to other backgrounds. In fact, Warners remade it in 1941 as a combat flick called *International Squadron* with Ronald Reagan as a wise guy Air Force pilot who causes a lot of grief until he is turned into an effective fighting man.

One of my most respected and talented writer friends, John Michael Hayes (*Rear Window, To Catch a Thief*), believes in the usefulness of templates when plots come hard. He often tells the story of another writer, Borden Chase, who had blown a successful career in Hollywood with drink and made his comeback with one of the neatest "templates" of all time. He wrote the story and screenplay of *Red River* for Howard Hawks and didn't reveal until a much later interview with Richard Corliss that he had simply lifted the characters and storyline of *Mutiny on the Bounty* with the patriarch, John Wayne, substituting for Captain Bligh, his stepson, Montgomery Clift, for Fletcher Christian, and the cattle drive to Dodge City which culminates in Clift leading a mutiny against his father, following the same pattern as the *Bounty*'s goal to deliver breadfruit from the South Pacific to Great Britain.

Unfortunately, there were no schools of screenwriting when I was working in Hollywood. The writers in the Communist Party tried from time to time to meet members' requests for discussions of works in progress, but often these sessions degenerated into discussons of a project's political correctness. Those lucky enough to work with directors like John Huston, Garson Kanin, and Orson Welles could learn something from their bosses. And I would suppose that the same holds true today for those who work with ex-writers like Lawrence Kasdan and Barry Levinson.

Movies are, after all, a story-telling medium and stories not only originate with writers, they are shaped and told by writers. So every screenwriting project is an adventure of sorts—as the following account of one writing assignment demonstrates.

Ad for Harry Rapf Productions. Page 110 of *Wid's Yearbook 1921–1922* (later called *Film Daily Yearbook.*) (Reprint from the author's collection, but made from a reprint by Arno Press, New York, in 1971.)

Scene from Harry Rapf Production of Wesley Barry in *Heroes of the Street.* The terrified little boy with the white scarf is Maurice Rapf, age 9 in 1923. (Photo from author's collection.)

Left to right: Harry Rapf, Louis B. Mayer, and Irving Thalberg behind the "key to success" at the dedication of the merged Metro-Goldwyn-Mayer Studio, April 1924. (Photo from the author's collection.)

Joan Crawford in a studio portrait by Ruth Harriet Louise, 1926. (Photo courtesy of the Robert Dance collection.)

Maurice Rapf, age 10, delivering fan mail to Norma Shearer on the MGM lot in 1924. (Photo from the author's collection.)

The Rapf Family in a comic studio portrait by Russell Ball, circa 1930. Standing left to right: Harry Rapf, Maurice Rapf, Matthew Rapf. Seated: Tina Rapf. (Photo from the author's collection.)

Left to right: Charles King, Conrad Nagel, and Cliff Edwards (Ukelele Ike) in a scene from the Harry Rapf Production *Hollywood Revue of 1929*. (Photo from the Museum of Modern Art Collection.)

Scene from Harry Rapf Production of *Min and Bill*, with Wallace Beery and Marie Dressler, 1930. (Photo from the Museum of Modern Art Collection.)

Left to right: Rabbi Edgar Magnin, Maurice Rapf, and Louise Seidel prepare for their wedding in January 1939. (Photo from the author's collection.)

F. Scott Fitzgerald (left) and producer Walter Wanger at Dartmouth Winter Carnival in 1939. (Photo from the author's collection.)

Malibu Beach CP Recruiting Party. Right to left: Paul Jarrico, Sandy Kibbee (later Ruben), Ring Lardner Jr., Pearl Slutzky, Richard Collins, Louise Rapf, Vicki Schulberg (age 2), and Jigee (Mrs. Budd) Schulberg (back to camera). (Photo from the author's collection.)

BY AUTHORITY OF THE HOUSE OF REPRESENTATIVES OF THE CONGRESS OF THE
UNITED STATES OF AMERICA

To ~~Hon.~~ William A. Wheeler

You are hereby commanded to summon ___Maurice Rapf___

to be and appear before the ___Committee on Un-American Activities or a___
___duly authorized sub-committee there of___
Committee of the House of Representatives of the United States, of which the Hon. ___

___Harold H. Velde___ is chairman. ___

Room 1105 Federal Bldg. New York, N.Y.
~~in their chamber in the city of Washington;~~ on ___May 4, 1953___

___, at the hour of ___10:30 A.M.___

then and there to testify touching matters of inquiry committed to said Committee; and he is

not to depart without leave of said Committee.

Herein fail not, and make return of this summons.

Witness my hand and the seal of the House of Representatives

of the United States, at the city of Washington, this

___18th___ day of ___April___, 1953

Harold H. Velde
Chairman.

Attest:

_____
Clerk.

Photostat of subpoena served on author in New York by
Federal Marshall on behalf of HUAC.

Producer Harry Rapf at his MGM desk in 1941. Note the plaster MGM lion and the picture of Maurice and Louise Rapf with their infant daughter, Joanna. A picture of Joanna can also be seen next to the telephone in the background. (Photo from the author's collection.)

Left to right: Harry Rapf, Harry Cohn, and Maurice Rapf strolling on the strand in Nice in 1925. (Photo from the author's collection.)

Left to right: Harry Rapf, Matthew Rapf, and Maurice Rapf with Buick in the back of Rapf's Lorraine Boulevard Los Angeles house, 1927. (Photo from the author's collection.)

Sunday picnic circa 1922. Standing and back row, left to right: Vera (Mrs. Joe) Rapf, unknown man, Joe Rapf, Irma (Mrs. Jack) Warner. Front left to right: Jack L. Warner, Jack Warner Jr., Maurice Rapf, Harry Rapf, Tina (Mrs. Harry) Rapf. (Photo from the author's collection.)

Louise Seidel (later Rapf) in a studio portrait while under contract to Paramount in 1937. (Photo from the author's collection.)

J. Blair Watson, founder of Dartmouth Film Society in 1949. (Photo courtesy of Nancy Wasserman, Montpelier, Vermont.)

Ralph Steiner, Dartmouth '21, photographer, filmmaker, and resident of Thetford, Vermont. (Photo courtesy of John Sheldon, Norwich, Vermont.)

Sam Moore, ex-President of Radio Writers Guild and long-time collaborator of Maurice Rapf. (Photo permission of Mrs. Chan Moore, Blairstown, New Jersey.)

Chapter 10

The *Winter Carnival* Story

Some people—many of my friends included—have the good fortune to be associated with one or more movies of quality. And, for them, it is a pleasure—although sometimes quite boring for others—to dig up the past and to explain how *Rear Window* (by John Michael Hayes), *On the Waterfront* (Budd Schulberg), or *The Graduate* (Buck Henry) came to be written. My fate is to be tied to a movie clinker named *Winter Carnival,* which is listed in December 1939 by the *New York Times* as one of the ten worst films of that year and a movie that is run almost annually on the Dartmouth campus, where I teach, because it immortalizes a traditional Dartmouth winter event. I could be asked about *Song of the South* or *Cinderella* (both of which I also wrote)—and I sometimes am—but, for some reason, curious movie buffs are more interested in the saga of the ubiquitous and now campy *Winter Carnival* than they are in anything else I wrote.

One reason why the story behind the making of the *Winter Carnival* is worth retelling is because that ordeal produced two literary offshoots: F. Scott Fitzgerald's unfinished novel about Hollywood, *The Last Tycoon,* published posthumously; and Budd Schulberg's *The Disenchanted,* a roman à clef about Fitzgerald that describes the latter's "lost weekend" at the scene of the carnival in 1939 and that was a Book-of-the-Month Club Selection in 1952.

From my point of view, the story begins with my marriage to Louise Seidel on January 5, 1939. It was a mixed-faith marriage and not accepted with much enthusiasm by my Jewish mother and father or by Louise's Lutheran-turned-Catholic mother, with whom she lived. When we announced to our respective parents on New Year's Eve that we planned to get married immediately, both mothers took to their beds instead of ringing in the New Year with good cheer. Nevertheless, the marriage took place at 1:00 P.M. a few days later before a small group of friends, limited in number to those who could fit around the dining room table for brunch in my parents' house.

The few days between the announcement and the event were marked by hustle and bustle. My brother Matthew, on vacation from Dartmouth on January 2, but not on the wedding day (the 5th), accompanied us to City Hall for the license and helped pick out the rings in a tawdry jewelry shop on Main Street near City Hall. There was a meeting with Rabbi Magnin, who would marry us, and I expected that he would ask for a number of commitments for conversion from my non-Jewish bride-to-be. I told Louise beforehand to agree to anything, that our objective was to consummate the marriage without a hitch, and that there was no way in the world the rabbi could make her live up to her promises later. As it turned out, the only promise he exacted was that she should raise her children as Jews and send them to a Jewish Sunday School. (And we kept that promise but made a deal with our three children about Sunday School: They would go for three weeks and then continue or not, as they chose. They all chose to quit, and only our oldest, Joanna, observes the Jewish holidays today.)

It was our intention to take off on a cross-country auto trip as soon as the marriage ritual and the midday meal were finished. Both Louise and I owned Plymouth convertibles, but mine was slightly newer so Louise sold hers and gave the cash to her mother. Since we had both lived with our parents, we had no houses to close up; we could leave on our trip with no strings attached. Except for one—Louise's dachshund. And we had made arrangements with a dog-loving friend to board Donna until we got back. But we had no idea when that would be. (Actually, after we had been sent off in a shower of rice—which it took three weeks to remove from our belongings—our first stop was at Louise's apartment, where we picked up the dog and delivered her to her temporary digs at Edith and Lester Ziffren's.)

Our combined savings at the time came to something like four thousand dollars and it was our plan to travel as far and as long as we could until that money ran out. I was twenty-four and Louise was twenty-two. When our money was gone, we would come back to L.A., rent a place to live, and find jobs in the movie industry. What we did, in fact, was draw all our savings out of our respective banks, pack everything we owned into the car, and take off.

That's where *Winter Carnival* enters and alters the picture. We had a wonderful trip across country. It was January so we took the southern route. In New Orleans, Louise was interviewed by the *Picayune* as a starlet, our pictures were taken, and I'm told by friends who have been there that they still hang on the wall at Antoine's famous restaurant.

We drove through Mississippi and Alabama to get to Miami, where I had some relatives and where we were treated with great courtesy by the president of MGM, Nicholas Schenck, and his wife, Pansy. As for Miami Beach, I hated it and haven't been back, lo, these fifty-eight years.

We had those wonderful WPA guidebooks with us. They were a product of the Federal Writers Project and used whatever highways existed as a thread on which to string the history of every nook and cranny of every state in the Union. One book was called *U.S. One,* and it followed that road from the Florida Keys to the Canadian border in Maine. We stayed with the book as far as New Haven, Connecticut, then turned off onto U.S. Highway 5, our destination being Hanover, New Hampshire, for the Dartmouth Winter Carnival in early February.

One must be a little nutty—or a really devoted alumnus—to take a bride all the way across country to celebrate a honeymoon at the Dartmouth Winter Carnival! But remember, this was supposed to be no more than a beginning to an extended holiday, modeled—though in a modest way—on the aspirations of Cary Grant in the then current movie adaptation of Philip Barry's *Holiday*. (In *Holiday* Cary Grant shocks his hoity-toity fiancée when he tells her he intends to make a million and retire at the age of thirty. She rejects him and he marries Katharine Hepburn, the fiancée's sister, who is delighted with the idea of an extended "holiday" when they are both young enough to enjoy it.)

Well, the trip to Hanover brought our holiday to an unexpected halt. There was a film crew there, shooting backgrounds for a proposed movie about Dartmouth called *Winter Carnival.* I had envied my friend Budd Schulberg, because he got the script assignment from producer Walter Wanger, who was in the class of 1915 at Dartmouth but left before graduation.

Now, after almost a year's work, Budd had not come up with an acceptable story and certainly not a screenplay. It was clear that the action would take place against the Carnival background and that one character in the movie would be the editor of the daily college paper, if for no other reason than because Schulberg had been the editor in his undergraduate days. It was also known that if they didn't shoot background material at the February 1939 Carnival, the movie could not be made until February 1940. And Wanger had already put himself in a bind by signing an agreement with Warner Bros. for the services of their rising star Ann Sheridan, who would report for work in April.

Faced with the need to expedite work on the story and script, Wanger hired the noted writer F. Scott Fitzgerald to collaborate with the novice Schulberg, and he brought both writers to Hanover to soak up the carnival atmosphere firsthand, to get started writing, and to advise the film crew which backgrounds to shoot. There is some reason to believe that Wanger hoped he would be rewarded by an honorary degree from the college he was about to immortalize and that he brought Fitzgerald to Hanover to help that cause and to show the literati on the faculty that he traveled in high-class company. Indeed, he invited the entire English department to a cocktail party in the Hanover Inn to meet the celebrated literary figure now working for him—and I was there.

Unfortunately, Fitzgerald, who was known to be an alcoholic but who had been on the wagon for several months, had been given a send-off on the flight east with a well-intentioned but devastating bottle of champagne, and when the time came for Wanger's party, the illustrious writer made his entrance by falling down the stairs leading to the Hanover Inn lobby. And that was just the beginning. He sobered up a little to make the trek up Main Street to the site of Outdoor Evening, where the Carnival Queen was crowned. (This ritual, subsequently considered degrading to women, was abandoned when the school went coeducational.)

Later, Fitzgerald insisted on making the rounds of the fraternities, where heavy drinking was de rigeur. The man who had celebrated decadent youth with his first novel, *This Side of Paradise* in the twenties felt very much at home with the decadent youth of the thirties. His usefulness to Wanger and the script, on the other hand, was at an end.

Here, the story is subject to two interpretations. Schulberg insists—and has so described it in his novelization of the incident in *The Disenchanted*—that Wanger fired both writers, that he (Schulberg) took Fitzgerald to New York and placed him in a drying-out establishment on the East Side, and that Wanger then rehired him. It was at this point—though this is not in the novel—that Schulberg was asked by Wanger to contact me as a collaborator. My recollection is that Schulberg was in Hanover and that he acted as intermediary between me and Wanger when I first turned down the offer because I was, in fact, on my honeymoon and didn't want to go back to Hollywood.

Wanger then offered to double my salary (I think this meant an increase from one hundred to two hundred dollars a week) and I think he said ~~that~~ Schulberg and I could stay in Hanover to work on the script. Wanger would be staying in New York for a couple of weeks to prepare for an appearance on the prestigious *Town Meeting of the Air,* a radio program carried nationwide, and we could confer with him there. My Hollywood agent thought it was a great opportunity, and my new wife regarded a stay in Hanover as an extension of our holiday, so I accepted.

Wanger was, at this time, angling to be president of the Academy of Motion Picture Arts and Sciences (which he became in December 1939) and enjoyed his role as a spokesman for the industry, but he liked to pontificate on international issues as well. As a movie producer, he was rather unique and traveled often in political circles. In fact, he was called on to help stage the launching of the United Nations in San Francisco in 1945. It is probable that he might have gotten the honorary degree from Dartmouth if ~~it had~~ not ~~been~~ for an unfortunate and unforeseen incident in Beverly Hills on December 13, 1951. His wife, the actress Joan Bennett, was rumored to be having an affair with her agent, Jennings Lang (a fact ~~that was~~ confirmed by a private detective hired by Wanger). One day, after spending most of the afternoon with Miss Bennett, whose car had been left in the MCA agency parking lot in Beverly Hills (where Wanger spotted it), Lang returned with his client, got out of his car, and was confronted by Wanger, who pointed a pistol at him and fired, hitting Lang exactly where he intended—in the groin.

In France, Wanger might have been given the *croix de guerre* for this crime of passion. In Southern California, after pleading not guilty by reason of temporary insanity, he was sentenced to four months on a work farm. It was the end of his role as spokesman for the industry, however, and, although he had one more fling at the big time as the first producer of the ill-fated Fox production of *Cleopatra,* he never attained his previous standing. What he did do, as a result of his encounter with criminal justice, was produce an inexpensive movie for Allied Artists, *Riot in Cell Block Eleven,* which was a clarion call for prison reform.

I saw him often in New York in the sixties and actually drove him to Dartmouth in 1970 when my class was celebrating its thirty-fifth

✳ – SAME YEAR AS "THE DISENCHANTED"

reunion and sponsoring a seminar on world peace in which Wanger shared the platform with General James Gavin.

My recollection differs from Schulberg's as to how the work on *Winter Carnival* proceeded. I recall that we started work in Hanover, having adjoining rooms in the Hanover Inn, and ~~that~~ at the end of the first week, Wanger got "antsy" and felt ~~that~~ we had to be in New York so he could confer with us every day. He was staying at the Waldorf; he booked rooms for us at the less deluxe (and less expensive) Warwick. Whenever we "conferred" with him, he was distracted by phone calls and by discussions with the chap who was the ghostwriter for his upcoming *Town Meeting* speech on the topic "Has 20th-Century Civilization Helped Mankind." In short, Wanger seemed to find story conferences something of a nuisance.

Our stories coincide, however, as to what happened next. The day after the *Town Meeting* broadcast (which occurred February 16, 1939), in which he shared the platform with the noted international correspondent, former wife of Sinclair Lewis, and model for Katharine Hepburn's role in *Woman of the Year*, Dorothy Thompson, Wanger announced that he was returning to Hollywood. Since we were now making progress on the script—even though we had written only about twenty pages—we must go, too.

I objected strenuously. He was going back on his promise—first to let us work in Hanover, then to let us stay in the East to finish the script. I had interrupted a honeymoon to oblige him and had no place to live in Hollywood. My wife and I had all our belongings with us, including our car. He both threatened and cajoled. Where was my loyalty? I couldn't walk off an assignment. As for the car, he would ship it to Hollywood and ship it back to New York again when the job was finished. He would pay my wife's train fare and mine, of course, and pay for the two of us to return to New York when the job was over. We would be back where we were with more money in the bank for a longer stay in Europe. What could we lose? Little did we know!

My wife never forgot that train trip. Here we were, still on a honeymoon, and I spent all night, every night, in the drawing room adjoining ours, working with Schulberg on a screenplay. The only time I saw Louise was at meals and then she had to listen to our talk about the idiotic affairs of ex-carnival queen, Jill Baxter, and the renewal of Jill's romance with our idealization of a young college professor, who had time to chaperone fraternity parties and to officiate at Winter Carnival ski events.

The only positive aspect of the whole assignment was having an opportunity to work in Hollywood with Chuck Riesner, who had been hired by Wanger to direct and had been given the job of getting a script out of two ex-Dartmouth undergraduates who had not yet learned how to write for the movies. Chuck had been around the movie business since 1920 and had worked intimately with Charlie Chaplin and appears as his ring opponent in *The Kid.* We spent more time listening to his stories than we did trying to figure out how to unravel the tangled lives of our mythical undergraduates and their adult friends and advisers.

After about five weeks, we had a finished screenplay but we didn't like it very much and neither did Wanger. The trouble was, he had no suggestions for improvements. I did, but they would have required a complete rewrite and Ann Sheridan was due to come on board in about two weeks. Then the expense meter would begin ticking at a fast rate. Wanger decided that I had to be replaced by someone who could write a shootable script in a hurry. He didn't want a masterpiece; he wanted something he could shoot. Craft, not art.

By this time, all thoughts of going back to New York and resuming the holiday honeymoon were gone. Louise had gotten pregnant and had miscarried. We were deep into a new life in our rented house in Westwood Village. And I had taken on new responsibilities in the Communist Party. But Wanger fired me and Schulberg told him that if I went, he would go, too. That brought forth the old bromide— "You can't walk off a job."

In this case, Wanger added a new twist. Schulberg had been on the assignment for a year. Wanger claimed he had a major investment in him (which was ridiculous—it could not have been more than a few thousand dollars). Schulberg was—and this was true—the only remaining authority on life at Dartmouth, which was what the picture was about. And then came Wanger's twist—the zinger: "If you quit now, I'll see to it that you never work in Hollywood again." I always thought that Schulberg should have quit. The threat was meaningless, and Budd knew it. But he stayed. The movie was made.

The tentative credits were sent out by Wanger's office. My name wasn't on them. I asked to read the final screenplay. I hated it, but it wasn't too different from the one Budd and I completed a few weeks before shooting. I called my agent and asked for advice. "If you're entitled to credit, take it," he said. "It's a major film by a major producer and will be distributed by a major company (UA)." "But it stinks,"

I said. "It doesn't matter," my agent said. "No one will remember. And you need the major credit. Take my word for it."

I did, and settled the matter with the other writer who was a friend and didn't want a credit fight. I ended up with joint story and joint screenplay credit. And my agent was wrong. People *did* remember, and after the film was released I couldn't get a job for four months. I'd go out on a job interview and everything would be going fine un-til I was about to leave. Then the producer, my potential employer, would ask, "Didn't you work on *Winter Carnival?*" And my affirma-tive answer would kill the deal.

My agent would probably be right about the value of credits on most clinkers. But *Winter Carnival,* as one of the worst movies of 1939, was something special. The fact that generations of Dartmouth undergraduates have enjoyed the movie as a midnight attraction on scores of subsequent carnival weekends has helped to heal the wound to some extent, but I still cringe when a discriminating student asks somewhat incredulously after one of those midnight showings, "Didn't you work on *Winter Carnival?*" I did, and, as I said at the outset of this diversion, there were two literary offshoots of that experience: Budd Schulberg's *The Disenchanted* and F. Scott Fitzgerald's *The Last Tycoon,* which is told in the first person by the daughter of a movie mogul who attends an Ivy League college and introduces the tycoon to a local Communist organizer (for "daughter," read Schulberg or me and you've got the point).

I barely got to know Fitzgerald during his "lost" weekend in Hanover. But about a year and a half later—in September of 1940—I was working at 20th Century–Fox, had an office in a Spanish man-sion known as the "writers' building" and knew that Scott was in one of the offices on the first floor. (His assignment was to do a screen adaptation of a play by Emlyn Williams called *The Light of Heart,* which ultimately reached the screen as *Life Begins at 8:30,* but with no credit for Fitzgerald.)

I hesitated to barge in on him, but then I received the manuscript of Schulberg's first novel, *What Makes Sammy Run?* and was told that Fitzgerald was one of a few others who had received it. (We were asked to read it to give an opinion as to whether or not it would be construed as anti-Semitic.) I dropped in on Fitzgerald with the ex-cuse of discussing the Schulberg novel about Hollywood, and we did discuss it. He didn't think it was anti-Semitic, nor did I. Sure, Sammy was odious and he was a Jew, but there were lots of other Jews in the book, including the narrator, who weren't bastards. And there was a very nice—if slightly sentimental—back story about Jews on the East Side of New York that explained why some young Jews are so eager to get ahead.

It also turned out that Fitzgerald was working on a Hollywood novel of his own. He was, as a result, a bit condescending about Schulberg's work, and I guessed a bit miffed that the younger man had completed his Hollywood magnum opus before he finished his own. Scott's book was about a character like Irving Thalberg, for whom he had once worked. He knew about my family background and thought I must know a lot about Thalberg and the whole MGM crowd. I did, and he plied me with questions. He asked me to stay to have lunch with him that first day. He explained that he didn't like to go to the commissary. He had his sandwich and coke brought in. I could order whatever I wanted—except booze. He was on the wagon, had been for a year. (I had already heard that bit of good news from other sources and also that he was living with a British-born Hollywood columnist, Sheila Graham, and trying desperately to make enough money as a screenwriter to resume his once successful career as a novelist and short story writer.)

Thereafter, we met frequently and he pumped me for information about the old days at MGM. When I read *The Last Tycoon,* which was published posthumously (he died a few months after leaving Fox) and included his copious notes for a very melodramatic climax involving union gangsterism, which I felt sure he would never have used, I could recognize one scene in particular that was attributable to our lunchtime gabfests. It's the one where the producer's daughter, Celia Brady, arranges for Stahr (the Thalberg character with whom she is secretly in love) to meet a charismatic young Communist Party organizer whom she also admires. Fitzgerald added his own touches to this meeting, which ends in a fistfight, but the basis was clearly a story I had told Scott about the weekly visits of a "downtown" CP character to my parents' house. (His name was Stanley Lawrence and he turned out to be an FBI plant, but he later atoned for his duplicity by joining one of the International brigades in Spain, where he lost his life.)

The reason Lawrence came to our house—and stayed for breakfast—was to deliver Marxist literature that I was to distribute at unit meetings in the evenings. He frequently encountered my father, who would be on his way to work, and I introduced them to each other.

Seeing the beat-up Model A Ford parked in front of the house on so many occasions, my father was curious about Lawrence's identity. When he asked me, I gave him a rather colorful—though not entirely accurate—picture of Stanley's background, that he was a Czech refugee who had fled ~~from~~ his country when Hitler took over and, with help from left-wing friends (my usual euphemism for the CP), had made it to the United States where he became a kind of link between the Left in the United States and friends abroad. I did not mention the "Comintern" to my father, but it was my impression that Stanley was a Comintern representative in Los Angeles. I also did not say anything about the Marxist literature or about my job as literature director for a Hollywood CP unit.

I had, however, told my father enough for him to conclude that Stanley's weekly visits to the family manse should cease. Stanley was surely being followed and, even if I was in no way implicated in international espionage, regular visits by an obvious foreign agent would make it appear ~~that~~ I was. The next week when he saw Lawrence sprawled out on a damask love seat in the elegant, white carpeted living room that was my mother's pride and joy, he blew his stack and ordered Lawrence to leave. "I know who you are," he said, "and if you have any consideration for my son, you will stay away from him."

That was the story I told Fitzgerald, and it laid the basis for one of the most dramatic confrontations in his unfinished novel—the ping pong game and fight between movie producer Stahr and the Communist, Brimmer. In *The Last Tycoon,* Celia's father, Brady, is characterized as a once powerful figure in the company and now on the skids, a clear reference to my father, although Brady is the company's token Catholic, which implies a reference to MGM studio manager, Eddie Mannix.

Fitzgerald, who never made it in Hollywood, clearly learned a lot about it. And much of what he didn't know firsthand he found out by talking to people—including me. Actually, Fitzgerald's description of the in-fighting among studio brass derived from discussions he had had with me, with Schulberg, and many others. He handled this material with such accuracy and wit that one can only rue the fact that he wasn't able to complete what would probably have been the best book about Hollywood ever written. REALLY?

Twenty years after World War II, *The Last Tycoon* was made into a movie ~~which was~~ directed by Elia Kazan, written by Harold Pinter, and starring Robert De Niro. And, having mentioned that war, let me write about what Hollywood was like during that troublesome period.

lie-low,

Chapter 11

World War II

The outbreak of war caught Hollywood off-guard. It wasn't that people in the Hollywood community were unaware of world problems or that the Jews who ran the industry were not sensitive to Hitler's anti-Semitism. But the official industry policy, dictated in part by the lay-low stance of the Jewish Anti-Defamation League and a desire to retain as many world markets as possible, was to observe neutrality which was at variance with the general trend of thinking in the community at large.

Warner Bros., known as the Roosevelt studio, was the first company to make an anti-Nazi film—*Confessions of a Nazi Spy*—in 1939. After Britain and France honored their commitment to Poland and declared war on Germany in that year, Hollywood started to make pro-British films. This sudden boldness had something to do with the loss of the Axis markets, and it led to an attack on the industry by the House Un-American Activities Committee. That group stupidly attributed what they described as "interventionist movies" to a Communist influence in Hollywood when, in fact, the Nazi–Soviet pact (which preceded the German invasion of Poland) had caused the Communists to join those who wanted to keep the United States out of "foreign" wars. The isolationist America Firsters blamed the new antifascist boldness on the Jews.

The attack on Pearl Harbor and our declaration of war in December 1941 changed all that. The prevalence of isolationist, pacifist thinking had to be overcome, and film was to be used as a principal tool to accomplish this. There ensued a widespread mobilization of movie talent to do what it could do best: make movies. But this required that writers, producers, and directors accustomed to turning out story films as entertainment had to adapt themselves to nonfiction subjects—to the documentary. The objective was to explain why we were fighting and to whip up patriotism and support for our allies—including the previously hated Russians. Some of the films, including Hollywood director Frank Capra's famous *Why We Fight* series, are such flagrant propaganda that they are embarrassing to see today. But those were the days when MacArthur could say, "The hopes of civilization ride on the banners of the glorious Red Army."

To the British whose homeland was being bombed by Nazis after the fall of France, the war was already a battle for survival. Fortunately, they had developed (under the guidance of John Grierson) a skilled corps of documentary filmmakers who moved over from General Post Office sponsorship to the Crown Film Unit and started making morale-building films and films for international consumption—especially for the United States—that would help to win support for their cause.

The message of the first British films was "We can take it"—showing the courage of the people under fire and the dedication to war work and to sacrifice. Typical "stiff upper lip" stuff. One film was actually called *London Can Take It.* This certainly created sympathy abroad, but not confidence. So within a year and a half, the message switched to "We can dish it out." And you had films like *Target for Tonight,* which chronicled a successful RAF raid on Germany.

These pro-British documentaries were shown in commercial theaters in the United States, as were the propaganda films produced by U.S. agencies once we joined the war against the Axis powers. Every branch of the service and many government agencies had motion picture units. The Army Signal Corps, by tradition a military branch concerned with communications, had the pivotal job of making orientation and training films for the GIs. The West Coast head of the Signal Corps was a producer named Sam Briskin, then designated a colonel, as were most of the producers who joined the armed forces.

Shortly after war was declared, I went to see Briskin and asked to be taken in to his corps. He asked me what my draft status was. When I told him it was 3A (because I had a wife and child) he told me to come back when I was reclassified as 1A (I never was.) He already had too many volunteers who were subject to the draft. I could at any time have enlisted for service as a private in the army or a gob in the navy, but, dedicated as I was to serving my country to help win the war against the fascists, I wanted to do what I thought I could do best—namely, to write movies.

Before the war ended, I had volunteered for the Army, the Navy, the Marine Corps, and the OSS. I was turned down by all of them, ostensibly for physical reasons, although I suspected it was because of my left-wing politics. In any case, I ended up doing writing jobs for the Industrial Incentive Division of the Navy (morale-building movies for defense workers) and for Nelson Rockefeller's Office of Inter-American Affairs (on helpful subjects like how to purify water for Latin Americans, the idea being to win support for the Allies instead of for the Nazis, who already had a foothold in Argentina).

At one point I went for an interview by a naval officer in downtown Los Angeles. At that time, I was up for a commission in the Industrial Incentive Division. Having had a number of turn-downs for legitimate physical reasons (such as a deviated septum), I prepared myself for this interview by spraying my nasal passages thoroughly with neo-synephrin so that I could breathe freely and a Navy medic wouldn't be aware of my problem. Unfortunately, no sooner had I settled in a chair across the desk from my Navy interviewer than he asked, "Are you a member of the Communist Party?" I was so stunned I didn't know what to say. What I did say—to my everlasting regret—was "No," which was stupid because the Navy obviously had agents who knew that I was still in the Party and, from what I subsequently learned about the attitude of the services to those who were known as Communists, membership in the Party would not disqualify me. Lying, on the other hand, did.

The closest I ever came to a legitimate and full-time government appointment was ruined by poor judgment on my part and by the assistance of some drunken friends. It happened this way: Budd Schulberg had been assigned to the OSS Film Unit headed by John Ford, a Navy commander. They needed a few writers who knew something about making movies, but when Schulberg came to Los Angeles looking for volunteers he got the cold shoulder. Ford then asked him, "What about that Communist friend of yours?" He meant me, and Schulberg called to ask if I wanted to work in the OSS unit with Commander Ford. Unlike the others, I agreed enthusiastically.

An official recruiter named John Abotti came to Los Angeles to formalize my appointment. He wore a Navy uniform; I think he was a two-striper, a lieutenant. We got along so well that I invited him to a stag party at my house that I was hosting for my brother Matthew, a naval ensign who was to be married the following day. Matt's friends were my friends, mostly sceenwriters and, unfortunately, very partial to booze. By eleven o'clock at night, the stag party had gotten pretty raucous. A faction of the guests, led by the well-known screenwriter Dalton Trumbo, decided that the time had come to attack the bridegroom-to-be and to shave his genital region. There was another faction who chose to come to my brother's defense, one of whom was John Abotti. The defense was successful, but the attackers got to Abotti, removed his Navy trousers, and started to spray his genitals with shaving cream. Grabbing his trousers, he ran in terror from my house.

Needless to say, I was not recruited by the Navy branch of the OSS. So I continued to work in Hollywood, frustrated by the idea that I was not participating fully in the most important event of our time, but doing what I could, usually under the aegis of an offshoot of the Writers' Guild, the Hollywood Writers Mobilization. Actually, there were some rewarding experiences on the home front. My work for Rockefeller's Office of Inter-American Affairs led to a collaboration with the noted German writer Lion Feuchtwanger (*Jew Suss, Power*) who was one of the colony of German exiles living in Pacific Palisades.

Car pooling to go to work was a necessity because gasoline was rationed, and I pooled with notables from West Los Angeles to Burbank when I worked at Warner Bros. in 1942. In the car pool were William Faulkner, John Huston, Jerry Wald, and proletarian novelist I. A. Bezzerides. Other luxuries had to be abandoned as well. We switched from butter to oleo-margarine (which was purchased in its original white form and could be converted to imitation butter-yellow by kneading it with a yellow powder). Sugar was rationed, imported liquor was unobtainable, meat was limited, worn-out tires were retreaded, and we went to the Red Cross blood bank every three months.

An office of War Information was established, and an ex-newspaperman named Lowell Mellett set up shop in Hollywood to advise studios on useful war-supportive subjects as well as to goose them into making them. This office also worked out a deal with the distributing companies to include government-made propaganda films in theaters. One piece of information that is worth noting and is seldom mentioned is that the movie industry, unlike any other in the country, served the war effort in many ways without being reimbursed—even on a cost-plus basis. It produced 16-millimeter prints of feature films and made them available to military bases and ships at sea, free of charge. (It should also be noted that this generous gesture opened the way for a profitable postwar market for the distribution of films in 16-millimeter, a new market that prospered for many years until the wide acceptance of films on videotape.)

No war up to that time had ever been covered so completely by movie cameras. One film, *The True Glory*—a joint British-American project with two directors, Garson Kanin (U.S.) and Carol Reed (British), and not released until after the surrender of Germany—included the work of 1,400 Allied cameramen, 101 of whom were wounded and 32 killed. One effect of showing war with stark realism is that it tends to become a statement against war. This was the opinion of the Army brass when they saw John Huston's film about the Italian campaign, *The Battle of San Pietro,* which not only included grim shots of battle but a painful scene of burial and of hundreds of white crosses. Told that the film might not be released because it was antiwar, Huston is said to have replied, "When the day comes that I make a movie that is *for* war, I ought to be taken out and shot."

Nevertheless, the Army added a prologue in which General Mark Clark explains the importance of the Italian campaign to justify the sacrifice of human life. No such simple solution was found for the release of another Huston army documentary, *Let There Be Light,* made in the Sawtelle, California, veterans' hospital to show—quite positively, as a matter of fact—the postwar psychological rehabilitation of brain-damaged GIs. The Army refused to let that film be shown publicly until a few years ago.

There has never been a time like that of World War II, in which the documentary played a role of such importance. It was the visual supplement to the main communications medium of the era—the radio—which brought us an analysis of day-to-day events, eyewitness accounts of battles and bombings, and all of Hitler's and Churchill's major speeches. Later, this material would find its way onto film, and documentary films would begin to assume their place as the predominant media for recording history.

In due time I would learn how to write documentaries. In the meantime, I had to learn how to write in a variety of styles for the movie medium.

Chapter 12

Animation and Disney

There can be typecasting of writers, as there is of actors. You write a hit Western and you are a Western writer, a hit whodunit and you're a mystery writer. The fact is that most movie writers, if they're worth their salt, can write anything. But being "typecast" sometimes helps to land a job.

Without a "hit" on my record, I became known as a "youth" writer. It is true that my first movie story had been *Divorce in the Family*, about the impact of a second marriage on a youngster, played by eight-year-old Jackie Cooper. My agent subsequently got me a job at Columbia on a story about juvenile delinquents, at Paramount on one of the Henry Aldrich (high school) series. This resulted in my doing a film about young unemployed actors taking over an abandoned theater and staging their own show in *Dancing on a Dime. Jennie*, at Fox, was about a young girl's rebellion against her martinet father.

So it was that Walt Disney wanted me to work on his movie about Uncle Remus. After all, it would be a story about a black man with storytelling skills and his relationship with a young white boy. Youth again. Nevertheless, when my agent told me of a possible job at Disney's, I balked. "How the hell can I write cartoons? And if I could, what good would it do my career? Better to be known as a 'youth writer' than a 'cartoon writer.'" But I was scheduled to go into the Navy—the Industrial Incentive Division—in about six weeks. I wouldn't be on the Disney payroll very long. So I agreed to go to the interview in cartoonland. And it turned out that the interview was with Disney himself.

He wanted me to work on what was intended as his first live-action film, based on the Uncle Remus stories that were written by a white Atlanta journalist, Joel Chandler Harris. He had bought a film treatment by an inexperienced southerner, Dalton Reymond, who had never written a screenplay, and Disney felt that Reymond needed a collaborator. I told Disney at our first meeting that I had misgivings about the Remus subject because it would sustain the "Uncle Tom" stereotype that leaders of the black community (such as the NAACP) were trying desperately to combat.

"That's why I want someone like you to work on it," he said. "You're against the black stereotypes. Most of us—even if we have no racial bias—commit booboos that offend people all the time. Because you are sensitive to the problem, maybe you can avoid it. I think Remus is a great character, a strong character. He is the dominant force in the story. There is no reason for Negroes [that was the word used then] to take offense."

It happens that I had boned up on the subject before going to the interview. The Remus stories about Brer Rabbit, Brer Fox, and company are part of American folklore. A popular reference book at the time was B. A. Botkin's *Treasury of American Folklore.* Harris's Remus stories are included. In his introduction to the stories Botkin explains that Harris had a unique knack for recreating in the original dialect the stories that he had heard from elderly blacks when he was a child. And then, most encouragingly for me, he invoked the words of a folklore authority named Peter Harwood as follows: "Whether quaint or stark, Negro animal tales project the compensatory dreams of the subject races and serf populations, expressed both in folk tale and ballad [which] delight in the victory of the weak over the strong and in the triunph of brains over brute stength." To which, Botkin added, "The way in which the Negro, more peculiarly than any other minority group has made this symbolism his own and a vehicle for his philosophy constitutes one of his most important contributions to folk literature and wisdom."

What this meant to me was that the undersized Brer Rabbit was a symbol of the oppressed black man who must use brains rather than brawn to outwit his more powerful masters. (In *Song of the South,* however, Brer Rabbit is presented as the alter ego of the little white boy played by Bobby Driscoll.)

I cannot defend *Song of the South* against those who find it racist. I know that it was picketed by the NAACP. I had to face a representative of that organization in a left-wing roundtable discussion after its release. I made it clear that there was a conscious attempt on Disney's part to avoid fostering black stereotypes. (I did not mention that Disney thought the attack on the picture was incited by Clarence Muse, who, as the reigning "serious" black actor in Hollywood, thought he would get the Remus part and resented the fact ~~that~~ it went to an unknown Easterner—a performer on the generally disliked Amos and Andy TV show, Jim Baskette.)

What I learned at that roundtable was that certain subjects—even though they may be accurately and fairly presented—can have a destructive effect if, at the time of their presentation, they seem to reinforce some demagogic concept. I understood this in terms of Budd Schulberg's *What Makes Sammy Run.* Was his book anti-Semitic because Sammy was a despicable Jewish character who climbs to the top at the expense of all his friends? I didn't think so. Hitler's propaganda minister, Joseph Goebbels, apparently did. I was told that Goebbels pirated the book and printed several hundred thousand copies for distribution to the German people to substantiate the Nazi concept of the unscrupulous Jew.

Song of the South was released at a time when the leaders of the black community were launching a struggle for recognition and civil rights. That struggle goes on, but it has made enough progress so that *Song of the South* can be released today without protest. And *What Makes Sammy Run* has taken its place as one of the best pieces of fiction ever written about Hollywood; but in 1940, with the Nazis justifying the elimination of six million Jews, it could be construed as anti-Semitic propaganda. (Warner Bros. is now considering production.)

Bad mouthing Disney—now that he is gone—has become something of a popular sport. One recent biography by Marc Elliot entitled *Hollywood's Dark Prince* actually alleges that Walt was a secret agent for the FBI and an anti-Semite. Maybe so, but I doubt it. He was certainly a conservative and was a frequent sponsor and joiner of conservative organizations. But when I worked for him as the war was coming to a close, he knew very well ~~that~~ I was a dedicated left-winger. He may even have known ~~that~~ I was a Communist. He certainly knew ~~that~~ I was Jewish.

Yes, Disney was a conservative when I knew him, and we found ourselves on opposite sides of many current issues. I once asked him what made him such a dyed-in-the-wool Republican. He told me ~~that~~ his father was, in fact, a Socialist, and very much opposed to Missouri's Democratic Pendergast machine. During one election campaign he was accosted by a bunch of young Irish toughs, offspring of Democratic machine supporters. Who was he for? they asked. He didn't know. In his family, either one of the two major parties was as bad as the other. But this group wanted to make sure he took the right message back home: "Vote the Democratic ticket." And, according to Disney, when the gang of young Democrats coated his balls with hot tar, he became a Republican for life. I am not sure I believe that story, but that is what he told me.

In one area Disney lined up with progressive elements: He appeared to be an early environmentalist. He believed in supporting the "balance of nature," and somewhere in my files I still have the pamphlet he gave me that made it clear that any act of man that interfered with natural processes (the use of insecticides, for example, or the unnatural protection of one animal species at the expense of another) was to be avoided at all costs. When he was attacked for the violence in some of his True-Life nature films—spiders swallowing flies, snakes swallowing mice, and so forth—he relied on the balance of nature as a defense. He actually purchased a novel, *The Woodcutter's House* by Robert Nathan, for me to adapt. The protagonist of Nathan's book was a little green man who tried to preserve the forests from the ravages of man, as specifically represented by lumber companies.

Another odd aspect to the Disney personality—at least, as I knew him—was his failure to recognize his own importance. This may have been an "act" on his part. After all, his outer office was lined with Oscars and the inner office had framed tributes from world leaders. But one day when we were discussing a live-action movie in which there would be no roles for big stars (it was actually the aforementioned *Woodcutter's House*), he said he couldn't go through with it. No chance to put important names in the cast. When I tried to point out that his name was one of the three best known in Hollywood (the others were Garbo and Chaplin), he shook his head. "Mickey Mouse maybe," he said, "not Disney."

I had planned to work at Disney's for six or seven weeks and ended up working there for two-and-a-half years after the war. My long stay came about after I had been fired from *Song of the South*. It happened like this: I was still working with Dalton Reymond and was about to start a second draft of the screenplay when I got a mysterious telephone call from a girl who asked me whether I had talked to my contact at Warner Bros. about getting a screen test. I was totally baffled by her question and wanted to know who she was. She was equally baffled by my bafflement and wanted to know who I was. I told her.

"But you don't sound like the Maurice Rapf I have been talking to," she said. "That's because I am certainly not the Maurice Rapf you have been talking to. So I think you had better come upstairs and we will try to straighten this out." I told her where I was—in the office of a veteran Disney associate and friend of mine, Ted Sears—and she did indeed come up. When she entered Ted's office, she looked around blankly, obviously not seeing anyone she knew. "I'm Maurice Rapf," I said. "Not the Maurice Rapf I know," she said, more confused than ever.

We figured out what had happened. My collaborator, Dalton Reymond, a married man, had been seeing this girl—a studio messenger—and promised to use his influence to get her a screen test at Warners. To avoid exposure, he used my name. I went to the producer of the film, a man named Perce Pearce, told him the whole story, and said I could no longer work with Reymond. Either Reymond went or I went. Pearce chose to keep Reymond, who had written the original story on which our script was based. I was fired that day—a Friday. I was rehired the following Monday by Walt Disney himself to work on a script of *Cinderella* with his reliable story man and my friend, Ted Sears. The picture was put into production some years later and released in 1950.

One of the problems Disney had early in the war was that the studio he had founded was on shaky footing. *Snow White* had been a great success, but he plowed the profits back into the company and built his grand new plant in Burbank, borrowing money to complete it. He followed *Snow White* with the very expensive *Fantasia,* which required rewiring many big city theaters for his wraparound sound system. Critics liked the movie. The public didn't. The public didn't much like *Pinocchio* or *Bambi* either. Of all these early features, only *Dumbo,* produced on a modest budget, made any money.

The creditors of the studio had insisted that the main building be readily convertible to a hospital in case of financial failure or a war. Now it looked as if Disney was faced with both when, unexpectedly, he was saved by the war itself and a host of government contracts to turn out lively animated subjects that would build morale and provide instruction. He and a corps of artists even made a trip to South America to make a goodwill movie (*Saludos Amigos*) for Rockefeller's Office of Inter-American Affairs. There was also the full-length feature of Sikorsky's book, *Victory through Air Power.* The Disney Studio became a defense plant and it survived.

But as the war came to an end and no animated theatrical feature had been made in three years, Disney decided to hedge his bets and move into live action. *Song of the South* was his first live action venture, although the Brer Rabbit stories were animated and there were some spectacular combinations of live characters in animated backgrounds and vice versa (and this was forty years before *Roger Rabbit*).

I had written a *Song of the South* screenplay for Disney and, because the Rabbit stories were integrated with the plot, I even wrote the animation sequences in screenplay form, though what finally appeared in animation bore little similarity to my written material. Disney, however, was not used to seeing his stories in written form. Members of his staff had inventive story minds but they were artists, and every short and every feature had been prepared in storyboard form—basic illustrations of action, with description and dialogue attached. I came to admire the storyboard method because you got a chance to test your concepts visually. Disney, on the other hand, began to see the advantages of the screenplay method. Why waste effort on artwork until you had developed the story and scene structure, the dialogue and routines?

After finishing the first draft (with Ted Sears) of the *Cinderella* screenplay (Disney's first postwar animated feature), I thought it was time for a storyboard, but he didn't agree. We had some lovely character sketches by the talented Mary Blair but that was all of the artwork extant on what was to be, after all, a product of artists as well as writers. Disney wanted our most recent script to hang around the studio for a while. Let the directors and animators mull it over, think about it. In due time, we'll go to it, he said.

That's how it always was with Disney. He taught me one wonderful but maddening lesson about the creative process: *Whatever you think you have done well, you can do better.* But he was wise enough to end every conference on a positive note. "Well, I think we've finally licked it." The trouble was you'd get a call the following morning. He had another idea. It might be good; it might be lousy. But the neat can of beans was reopened. And you kicked it around some more. Maybe until lunchtime. Then you got the line, "I think we've finally licked it." Until later that afternoon.

I often wondered how he ever okayed a project for production. I knew that *Snow White* had taken seven years to produce, and I began to see why. But then I found out how final decisions were made. It happened on my third writing project for him, an adaptation of a children's book, *So Dear To My Heart.* The script was going through the usual sieve of refinement when it was announced that the Technicolor cameras for shooting the film were arriving the following Monday. That Friday, when Walt said, "I think we've finally licked it (or got it)," it was for keeps.

One other rather endearing Disney idiosyncrasy was his eagerness to foster a "one-big-happy-family" atmosphere at the studio. He insisted that everyone, even the fifteen-dollar-a-week office boys and girls, call him "Walt." He wanted everyone to eat in the studio commissary where he did a lot of table hopping. My buddies, all Disney veterans, refused to enter Walt's commissary, preferring, in their free lunch hours, to get out from under and to fortify themselves at neighboring watering holes.

The only times I stayed on the lot for lunch were on the days when old comedies were run in one of the studio "sweatboxes" (projection rooms). This was not just for fun, though fun it was. Animators and story men had much to learn from the old Mack Sennett comedies, from Chaplin, Keaton, Lloyd, and Charley Chase. Once in a while, they would run a "pencil test" (an animator's original drawings, rather than final renderings by ink and paint staff) of some work in progress.

It was said that Walt had originally hoped ~~that~~ the employees would live in a circle of houses surrounding the studio so they could walk to work. And he himself was said to bring his family to picnic on the grounds on weekends when he was not snooping around the administration building, peering in at the artwork on the walls of his artists' offices, and even going through the contents of waste baskets.

There were also a lot of studio sponsored family events. I had young children when I worked for Walt, and they enjoyed the monthly Saturday shows in the studio theater with entertainment and refreshments for the kiddies. I can also remember at least two studio picnics, one of which was held at artist Ward Kimball's house where there was a full-sized nineteenth-century train on a few hundred yards of track leading to a replica of an old station. Kimball was said to be making money with the train by renting it out from time to time to major studios, but on one occasion Walt Disney donned an engineer's hat and drove the engine back and forth, and our kiddies had a fine time. (Some years later, Walt made a live action film with a Civil War background, *The Great Locomotive Chase*, using Kimball's train.)

I haven't visited the Disney studio since the fifties, and most of the very talented people I knew there are retired or dead. Two of my former students got jobs there but left because there was so little room for advancement. And although animation—made more feasible today with computer-generated images—is making a noteworthy comeback at the box office, the new animation subjects, like so many of our current features, seem to me frenetic, nasty, and without charm. Maybe you liked *Aladdin.* Certainly, the animation tricks were spectacular, but special effects have always been notable in animation.

Animated short subjects have never been box-office bonanzas, even though their stars were frequently billed on marquees above the features they were intended to support. Thus, the thirties belonged to Disney's Mickey Mouse and Donald Duck, the forties to Merrie Melodies' Bugs Bunny, and the fifties to a couple of upstarts from United Productions of America with the near-sighted Mr. Magoo and Gerald McBoing-Boing (a precocious youngster who substituted sound effects for speech).

I am frankly no animation expert, but I have written a lot of animation scripts—during my years at Disney and for thirty years thereafter (the most recent being a CBS presentation, *Gnomes,* in 1980). Since I can't draw, I can't direct animation in the sense of supervising the preparation and shooting of backgrounds and the animation itself. But I have directed soundtracks for animation subjects that require the recording of a soundtrack before being turned over to animators, who match lip movement to speech and physical movement to footsteps, falls, slides, explosions and such. (This reverses the process of live action in which the "mix" of sound tracks is the final process before printing.)

Bear in mind that animated cartoons are the "purest" form of moviemaking since they are derived, not from a reproduction of elements in a real world, but purely from images conceived by and rendered by artists. Movement itself is manipulated and, since the late twenties, has been magically wedded to lively and ingeniously created soundtracks.

Animated drawings actually preceded motion pictures. The old flip book was drawn, and it could provide movement because of our persistence of vision, which holds the impression of an image momentarily while it is replaced by another. That master physicist-lexicographer who is also credited with the thesaurus, Peter Mark Roget, discovered the persistence of vision principle in 1824. Almost a hundred years later (in 1909), a comic strip artist named Winsor McKay drew thousands of pictures of a dinosaur and put them on film to simulate movement. A year or so later he traveled the country with a vaudeville act that is generally assumed to be the first succeful theatrical presentation of animation in motion pictures. The filmed part of the act was called *Gertie the Dinosaur.*

Although Winsor McKay made thousands of drawings to simulate real motion, some of his successors realized that even jerky motion could be interesting, so instead of sixteen drawings per second, they cut it down to twelve and then to eight and less. Not only that, but they soon figured out that they did not have to draw the background for each picture. The foreground character who moved could be on a separate cellulloid transparency (hence the word "cel") and laid over a drawn background that did or did not move. And that character might only have to be redrawn in part to move some of his limbs and not the entire torso. And if the figure was running or walking, there were only a few basic drawings that were necessary because they could be repeated in cycles while the background moved behind him or her. Yes, artists in the animation field were clever fellows, and they were quick to learn how to present their images of simulated reality efficiently and effectively.

What marks the difference between the simple matter of reproduction and genuine creative achievement is not the pretty picture but the content, although it's nice to have quality in both. New audiences may be enchanted by seeing a drawn character like a dinosaur turn its head and then reach up to catch an apple, but after a while they demand that the character have an objective, that some other character interfere with that objective. They want a story. When Walt Disney did his first synchronous sound short subject, *Steamboat Willie,* the audience was entranced by the synchronization of a stick producing the sounds of a xylophone by banging on the teeth of a cow and by Mickey's foot keeping perfect time to "Turkey in the Straw." But what made the cartoon work was that Mickey gave a boat ride to Minnie, that Peg Leg Pete tried to make out with her, and that Mickey saved her.

That was true of almost every cartoon Walt Disney ever made. They were often beautiful, they had good music, but they also had, as a basis for their gags and action, a simple story line. Donald Duck wants to spend a restful day at the beach, but is harassed by an annoying bee. Two pretty trees stand side by side in a forest and they love each other, but a jealous stump wants "in" and starts a forest fire to have his way. Two of the three little pigs submit to the entreaties of the "big bad wolf" and would be eaten alive if it weren't for the industrious third pig, who had the foresight to build his house of brick.

The chief criticism leveled at Disney—and it is one with which I agree—was that he began, after the success of *Snow White,* to concentrate too much on technical improvement. He never abandoned his concern for story content, and his fertile imagination was never satisfied with the first idea that came along. But he wanted to make animation lifelike. He succeeded so well in *Bambi,* with his multiplane camera adding actual depth to the forest, that one wag wondered why he hadn't made the movie with real deer.

By the time he made *The Sleeping Beauty* (1959) his artists had improved their animation techniques to such a point that even the movements of human figures (always a bugaboo for animators) were fluid and natural. This was accomplished by using a rotoscope to trace photographed movement of real people. But was this lifelike achievement necessary?

One talented group of ex-Disney artists didn't think so. They had left the studio after the devastating strike for recognition of the Screen Cartoonist's Guild in 1941, which had a traumatic effect on those who were faithful to Walt as well as on those who struck and ended forever the "family spirit" that Walt tried so diligently to keep alive. Some of the staunch unionists (John Hubley and Phil Eastman) served in Army motion picture units. Others (Steve Bosustow, David Hilberman, and Zack Schwartz) formed an independent company (which became United Productions of America) and did some highly successful shorts for the Armed Forces on modest budgets, thus going into competition with their old boss and mentor.

This group of ex-Disneyites (who eventually got together and attracted other talented people) saw the future of the medium to be a return to individual expression, unbounded by the constraints of realism. Or perhaps the lack of big budgets forced them to abandon naturalism in favor of a one-dimensional stylization. They drew no elaborate sets. A nonexistent wall could be suggested by hanging one picture, a staircase by a bannister but no steps. The audience filled in the rest.

They started on the "sponsored film" route with films for the armed forces, "message films," which led to *Hell Bent For Election,* paid for by the UAW/CIO as that organization's contribution to Roosevelt in the 1944 election. And then came *Brotherhood of Man,* another United Auto Workers public service project, on which I (moonlighting without pay from my job at Disney's) worked as one of the writers.

Their flat, stylized characters acting out stories against sketchy backgrounds were clearly a reaction against Disney's lifelike reproduction, and their popularity led to a contract with Columbia Pictures. There, innovation led to literary adaptations like that of Ludwig Bemelman's charming children's classic, *Madeline,* Thurber's *Unicorn In The Garden,* Poe's *The Tell-Tale Heart,* and a free-wheeling version of the Frankie and Johnny legend, *Rooty Toot Toot.* Disney had dominated the cartoon field for twenty years, winning dozens of Oscars, but most of the Academy Awards for animation in the early fifties went to UPA, to McBoing-Boing, Magoo and company.

Some Disney artists, notably the talented Ward Kimball (who headed a jazz combo of Disneyites called "The Firehouse Five"), went to Walt and asked for permission to do a little avant garde animation on their own (anyone who has seen the "Pink Elephants" number from *Dumbo* needs no proof of Disney artists' capabilities in this sphere). The result was a unique cartoon in Cinemascope, *Toot, Whistle, Plunk and Boom,* done in the flat UPA style, only better, and it was the Academy Award–winner for 1954. Kimball came to Disney the next day in triumph with an idea for a follow-up. "Forget it," Walt said. "We've proved we can do it. Now let's get back to what we do best."

By this time, of course, the Disney production machine was in high gear and undergoing vast changes. There were three live-action features being made for every full-length animation. Disney had jumped into TV from the very beginning with his Mouseketeers, in which he himself appeared weekly. And the first Disneyland was under construction in Anaheim. UPA, with its Gerald McBoing-Boing and Mr. Magoo, thrived for a couple of years and then, like Mickey Mouse and other distinguished predecessors, were gobbled up by the mass production of TV programming, including the Saturday morning kiddie shows, many of them produced overseas at a lower cost than is possible in the United States.

The Disney company has—until recently—remained aloof from this trend. It even has its own cable network to parcel out gems from its vast and rich library. But one of the great creative incubators in the film capital has turned into a vast corporate enterprise. The master is dead. The company is in new hands, and it is one of the most successful in Hollywood. But some of the old magic is gone.

I left Disney early in 1947. I had been there two-and-a-half years, and, because most of my writer friends at other studios had been climbing the salary ladder, I wanted a raise. Disney wouldn't give it to me unless I became a producer or a story editor, which I considered a negative reflection on my ability as a writer. So I left.

Whether I would have been fired later in the year when I was named as a Communist at the hearings of the HUAC, where Disney appeared as a friendly witness, I will never know. He certainly knew about my politics when I worked for him. Whether he would have bucked the blacklist to keep me on is another question—as is what I ultimately did to survive the blacklist itself.

Chapter 13

The Blacklist

I am often asked to talk about Hollywood in the fifties not because I was there but because I wasn't. I left Hollywood before the fifties began for a number of reasons, not the least of which was that I had been a member of the Communist Party, that I had heard I was to be subpoenaed, and that I didn't want to answer questions. I was—during the fifties—no longer a member of the Party nor a part of the Hollywood community, but my association with both continued to play a major role in my life and has continued to do so ever since.

Even though I left the Party in the mid-forties, I have always believed that the paranoia of anti-Communism, which made the fifties' blacklist possible, has been used as an excuse for some of the worst skulduggery of our time—and has been the justification for enormous defense expenditures and for constant meddling in the affairs of third world countries.

I was a member of the Communist Party for a bit more than ten years, weathering some difficult crises involving the Soviet Union, which was supposed to be the beacon light of progress to a Communist like me. How, one might ask, did I rationalize the Moscow purge trials of 1937? (I believed the Trotzkyites were plotting with the Nazis to undermine the socialist experiment). How did I accept the Nazi-Soviet Non-Aggression Pact of 1939 which led to the Nazi invasion of Poland and the start of World War II? (I had a hard time with this but became convinced that Stalin was just buying time to prepare for the subsequent Nazi invasion of the Soviet Union, which, in fact, was what Churchill and his European allies had wanted all along.)

To this day, I don't know the correct answer to all the questions. But membership in the Party in Hollywood brought me into close re-

lations with interesting people who shared my somewhat illiterate
Marxist view that capitalism was doomed, that by evolution or revolution the exploitation of workers by employers would give way to a
more equitable distribution of wealth whereby workers would indeed
get the benefit of their labors. The irony is that U.S. workers—at
least, those who were organized in unions—*did* get an increased
share of the wealth they produced and by the mid-sixties clearly belonged to the middle class. In this same period, the standard of living
for the Soviet worker was stagnant and, by the time alterations in the
socialist system were proposed by Gorbachev, access to food, cloth-
ing, and luxury items had actually declined.

Now we gloat at the demise of Communism in Eastern Europe,
and the Iron Curtain that separated us from the evil empire of the Soviet Union seems to have fallen. What this means, of course, is that
we will have to find new bad guys, new scapegoats to justify wars, to
justify infringement on civil liberties and cutbacks in necessary social
legislation (now called "entitlements") in favor of defense spending.
At first, I thought that the new "heavies" would be the drug lords or
alleged terrorists, and then we got Hussein. Now, along with that dis-
traction, we have Bosnia and the Middle East. We also have Castro's
Cuba to kick around, as well as assorted guerilla movements in Peru,
Salvador, Colombia, Guatemala, and a few African countries.

I realize that many readers may disagree with my deeply felt con-
viction that anti-Communism has been a principal cause of mischief
in this troubled modern world. But remember that anti-Communism was the justification for involvement in Korea, Vietnam, El Salvador, Chile, Nicaragua and Grenada. And disguised as antiliberal-
ism, it helped to give George Bush a landslide victory over Mike
Dukakis. I certainly don't expect to change anyone's opinion. My intention is merely to give you an impression of a period—the fifties—
when this hysteria about the "red menace" reached an unprecedented
peak and had a profound effect on my life, on the nation as a whole,
and, in line with our concern, on the film industry and the movies
that were made at that time.

Actually, I left Hollywood in 1947, a month before the much-pub-
licized hearings of the House Un-American Activities Committee began its investigation of Communism in movies, and in which ten witnesses, most of whom were friends of mine, refused rather vociferously
on the grounds of the First Amendment to reveal their political affiliations and were then cited for contempt of Congress. Two years later,

after a protracted legal battle that ended in the Supreme Court, these men, known as the "Hollywood Ten," went to prison. The industry spokesmen (including L. B. Mayer, Jack Warner, and Eric Johnston, head of the MPAA) who had at first challenged the allegations, responded to the adverse publicity and intimidation and instituted a blacklist of suspected Communists. And the committee, renewing its hearings in the fifties, dug up a sufficient number of informers to provide the industry with several hundred names that were to become unemployables.

In 1948 I took refuge from the inquisition by moving to Norwich, Vermont, across the Connecticut River from Dartmouth College, where some of my friends on the faculty were having their own problems with a New Hampshire state investigation of alleged subversives—brought on, in part, by their active campaigning for the Progressive Party, which nominated Henry Wallace for president in 1948.

As the fifties began, one by one, my Hollywood friends were called before the committee. A few cooperated and answered what the 1947 chairman, J. Parnell Thomas, had called "the $64 question"—"Are you now or have you ever been?" If they answered affirmatively, they had to give names of fellow members. And some did. One character—whom I had never considered a friend—named 162 people, including me. Others, to their credit, refused to cooperate but, because of the failure of the First Amendment to protect the Hollywood Ten, chose to take refuge in the Fifth Amendment (which protects a witness against self-incrimination) and were immediately branded as "Fifth Amendment Communists" and no longer able to work.

I was fortunate and, though frequently subpoenaed, never appeared before the committee. During the years I spent in Norwich, Vermont, I was never approached by the committee's agents or by the FBI. I thought that they had lost track of me, a fact that was disproved when I got my dossier from the FBI under the Freedom of Information Act a few years ago.

You may rest easy about the efficiency of your government snoops. If my file is indicative, the FBI spares neither time nor expense in keeping tabs on alleged public enemies. They had tracked my every move since 1934 when I went to the USSR as a summer student, relying on a variety of informants for their information. I know this because in the document I received, the names of the informants, providing such information as "attended meeting of a Progressive Party

caucus at the home of Professor so-and-so on Elm Street," are care-
fully blacked out. The name of the professor was not blacked out,
but—though it would mean nothing to the readers of this text—I
won't name names, even today.

My file for this period includes reports from FBI offices in Los Angeles, in Concord, New Hampshire, in Rutland, Vermont, and in
New York City. That's where I went in 1951, and two weeks later my
doorbell rang and two strange characters showed me their badges and
said they had come to ask me some questions. Foolishly, I talked to
them quite freely about my own activities of which they were fully
aware—but refused to answer questions about others.

Shortly thereafter, within a few weeks of my move to New York
City, I was subpoenaed to appear before the House Un-American Activities Committee at hearings to be held in New York's Foley Square.
I remained on call with one subpoena or another until 1956. It was
a period of constant harassment, fear, and uncertainty, even though
there were times when I received support from unexpected sources.
Consider that first subpoena as an example. It arrived like a blow
from a sledgehammer—at dinnertime, with my three small children
(the oldest was ten) seated around the dinner table demanding an ex-
planation for the pink sheet that I brought back after answering the
door.

I was to appear before the House Un-American Activities Committee the following Monday at 9 A.M. in Foley Square. A few phone
calls revealed that most of my friends in New York, who, like me, were
expatriates from Hollywood, had also been called. During the next
few days, we conferred separately with attorneys, and some of us who
had opposed the actions of the committee in the past actually met as
a group with an attorney on Sunday night to discuss strategy—the
principal question being whether to invoke our First Amendment
right to privacy of political belief (which had not kept the Hollywood
Ten out of jail) or to use the Fifth Amendment's protection against
self-incrimination, which had been used successfully by mob boss
Frank Costello when Senator Estes Kefauver tried to nail him. Our
attorney—who, like everyone else involved in this ordeal, shall be
nameless—strongly urged the Fifth Amendment approach if we
wanted to defy the committee and still stay out of jail. But to be perfectly frank, I left the Sunday night meeting totally unsure of what
answer I would give when the committee put the screws on.

Fortunately, although I was as clearly identified for the blacklist as if I had appeared, I never did have to testify before the committee. The Monday morning of that first hearing I woke up with a nasty sore throat. When I went to gargle, I was appalled by my image in the bathroom mirror. My cheeks were swollen preposterously like someone with the mumps, a childhood disease I never had. From the looks of my face, I had it now.

We were living in a sublet furnished apartment on West 86th Street and had only been in New York for about three weeks. We had no family doctor to call so my wife got dressed, went down to the lobby of the apartment building, and looked at the framed directory. There were three doctors in the building. She chose one Jules Boruchowitz because he lived on the floor above us. He confirmed that I had the mumps and at my age (thirty-seven), mumps could create a problem. (He was referring to something I knew very well—that mumps, though harmless for children, could be a potential source of impotence for an adult.)

I said, "I may have a problem, but you have one, too." And I told him about the HUAC subpoena, that I was due in Foley Square in an hour, that the committee personnel would never believe that a thirty-seven-year-old man developed a case of mumps the first morning of the hearings, and that he could be sure they would ask him to verify his diagnosis.

This didn't seem to faze him at all. "You have the mumps, there's no question about that. Not a very bad case, but the mumps just the same." "How long will I be confined?" I asked. "How long do you think the hearings will last?" he asked. "About three weeks." "Then I would testify that you will be confined to bed for at least three weeks."

I called my lawyer, who reported the information to the committee counsel, who called Boruchowitz for confirmation, but, unsatisfied, said that they would send their own doctor to examine me. Boruchowitz told me not to worry. His diagnosis of my mumps was accurate. He was also correct in saying that I had a light case. By the end of the week, all of my symptoms had disappeared. No sore throat, no puffed-up cheeks, no fever, nothing. And still no visit from the committee doctor. Not only that, but the hearings were proceeding at a snail's pace. They would last more than three weeks.

At the end of the third week, the hearings were still going and I still had not had a visit from the medical rep of the committee. I knew that if he came now, he would find me fit as a fiddle and ready for the inquisition.

He showed up on the first day of the fourth week of hearings—a young naval ensign with a gold medic insignia above the one stripe on his sleeve. He had short-cropped blonde hair, blue eyes, and seemed a perfect specimen of the all-American boy. He had a sidekick cut from the same mold, presumably as a witness. I was sure my goose was cooked.

He asked me to open my mouth and probed around with a tongue depressor. What could he possibly find? I felt fine. "You've got the mumps all right," he said. "But I'd say the worst is over." I was astounded. "How long do you think I have to stay in bed?" I asked. Like Boruchowitz, he then asked: "How long do you expect the hearings to last?" This time I said I didn't know. What I did know—and know now—is that when you're in trouble, you find friends in strange places.

I found another friend a few years later when I discovered a note on the door to my apartment. "Please call the U.S. marshall (followed by a telephone number). He has a subpoena for you." Having been so gratuitously warned, I packed a bag, picked up my wife, and headed out of town, to remain incommunicado until the next set of hearings in Foley Square were completed.

Bear in mind that during these escapes from the committee, the proceedings are being broadcast on the radio, either in their entirety or in excerpts on the news. Living in what is tantamount to a police state is consistently frightening. Even my wife was occasionally accosted on the street by well-dressed giants who were either FBI agents or agents of the committee. "Do you mind talking to us?" they would ask. She did mind.

Some of my Hollywood friends avoided this harassment by leaving the country. Some went to Mexico, some to England, some to France. But travel was not always so easy. Indeed, one of my worst "blacklist experiences" occurred when I tried to renew my U.S. passport in 1955.

I had a legitimate job with Transfilm, a company specializing in films for corporate sponsors in New York City. I had written and directed the soundtracks for two short animated films—one was *Calling All Salesmen* for *Life* magazine, the other was *Man Of Action*, a movie about urban renewal for the American Committee to Improve Our Neighborhoods. Both had been approved by the clients in storyboard form, and I had used well-known and exceedingly competent actors (including many who were blacklisted and unable to work when they were visible) as the voices of the animated characters.

Then, for reasons of economy, it was decided to finish the films in England. The director would be the blacklisted David Hilberman, then living in London but at one time the executive producer and owner of the successful Tempo Films, which was driven out of business by an attack in an anti-Communist publication, *Red Channels.* Hilberman would work with the staff of Halas and Batchelor, Britain's premier animation studio (responsible for the feature, *Animal Farm,* in 1954).

What caused my trouble was the decision to send me to England to work with Hilberman. I told the producer, the estimable Walter Lowendahl, who knew ~~that~~ I was a blacklisted Hollywood writer and ~~that I~~ had a passport which still had a few months to go if it was renewed—usually a simple operation requiring little time or fuss. I went to the passport office at 630 Fifth Avenue, filled out the necessary forms and turned over the passport (originally issued in Woodstock, Vermont) and was told that I should have it back within forty-eight hours.

When I turned up in forty-eight hours and went to the window where I had turned in the passport, I was told to go to an end window for special services. There I gave my name and the clerk went to an accordion-like folder and pulled out what I assumed was my passport to which was attached a white slip. He read the slip, looked over at me quizzically, and drew an eight-by-ten sheet of paper out of a drawer. Then, still holding my passport, he returned to the window where I was standing and shoved the eight-by-ten sheet of paper in front of me with his right hand, while holding the precious passport in his left.

"If you'll please sign this document," he said. "I need your signature before I can give you the passport." My heart was beating very rapidly. That precious passport was so near to me and yet so far. Because I knew even before I looked what I would see on that sheet of paper he wanted me to sign. There was a whole page of type but just above the space for my signature was the statement, "I am not now and never have been a member of_____." And I knew I couldn't—wouldn't—sign.

I told the man as much and asked if he objected to my calling a lawyer. He did not. I called the lawyer, who told me what I already knew—that I couldn't and shouldn't sign. But the lawyer also said ~~that~~ I should write to Washington to protest the insistence on a loyalty oath as a precondition for travel.

I wrote and received a reply from Frances G. Knight, Director of the Passport Office, dated June 14, 1955, which began as follows:

> I regret to inform you that after a careful consideration of your request for renewal of passport No. 497104 issued to you on August 15, 1951, the Department of State is obliged to disapprove your request. . . . In your case it has been alleged that you were a Communist, having been a member of the Young Communist League, Communist Political Association, and Communist Party.

I was informed that I could have a hearing, but the damage had been done. I had to tell my employers, who in this instance included the president of Transfilm, Billy Miesegaes, that I could not obtain a renewal of my passport. My immediate superior, Lowendahl, knew *why* and, fortunately, Miesegaes did not ask.

A month later—July 11—I wrote to the State Department canceling my request for renewal and pointing out that the arbitrary refusal to renew, which I regarded as unconstitutional, had forced my employers, at considerable expense, "to make other arrangements to carry out the work" I was supposed to do in London. I told my lawyer that I wanted to sue and take the matter to the courts. He pointed out that there were already several lawsuits against the State Department for failing to grant travel rights to people suspected of left-leanings (including Paul Robeson and the artist Rockwell Kent) and that I should wait for a decision by the Supreme Court on one of the pending cases.

I followed the lawyer's advice and was without a passport from 1955 to June 17, 1958, on which date I read in the morning *New York Times* that the Supreme Court had ruled against the State Department's use of the loyalty oath to deny passports to Rockwell Kent and one Weldon Dayton, on the grounds that such refusal of a U.S. citizen's right to travel was unconstitutional. The next day I went to 630 Fifth Avenue to apply for a new passport, and in the summer of 1959, with a new and legitimate passport, I went with my wife and three children on the *Queen Elizabeth* for a three-month tour of Europe. (When I was given the familiar form with the loyalty oath, I wrote, "Supreme Court Decision, June 16, 1958, as basis for not answering." And that apparently did the trick.)

One other serious encroachment on my civil rights occurred in 1955, when I was turned down for additional term insurance with the Metropolitan Life Insurance Company. I wrote to the president of the company as follows:

> I am insured under several policies with your company and in the past have never had any difficulty in obtaining insurance as I felt the need of it. Recently . . . at my direction, Mr. Brownstein [Metropolitan agent] submitted my application for an additional ten thousand dollars of insurance. After some delay, I was informed that the company could not find it possible to consider me for additional insurance and they could give me no satisfactory reason why I had been refused.

The agent had checked with the doctor who examined me. There was no medical reason for the turn-down. The agent asked me hesitantly, "Have you ever been in trouble with the law? Are there any moral grounds they could have?"

I knew, of course, why I had been turned down, and when I told the agent he was shocked. What it meant, however, was that, without a stated reason, I was to all intents and purposes uninsurable. Three years later, when the policies in force came up for automatic renewal, I asked again for the reason I was turned down and requested an opportunity to come in to discuss the matter. A Metropolitan third vice president wrote:

> I do not see that anything worthwhile would be accomplished by your taking the time to do so. . . . It has long been the settled policy of this company not to discuss the many underwriting factors that must be considered individually and collectively in arriving at our underwriting decisions.

In other words, they could turn me down but they did not have to say why. And when applying to another insurer (as I did to the N.Y. Savings Bank Life Insurance Fund) and they asked, "Have you ever been turned down for insurance?" I had to answer "yes" and consequently was turned down again.

I realize that there are people who say we got what was coming to us. There are others who choose to make heroes of us for not giving in to pressure. Some of us began to develop a holier-than-thou attitude, wearing our Joan of Arc mantles and feeling like martyrs. But it was no fun. When the blacklisted writer Dalton Trumbo received the Writers Guild Laurel Award many years later, he said there were no heroes or villains—only victims—a controversial statement with which even his wife disagreed. The fact is there were villains and, if there were no heroes, there were at least some people with the courage to abide by their principles. —BUT NOT SCHULBERG

We think of this period as the McCarthy era, but Senator Joe McCarthy simply capitalized on the paranoia for his own political ends. The "red menace" had been used effectively as an excuse to attack issues and people challenging the status quo after the success of the Russian Revolution. In the twenties we had the Palmer raids and the convictions of Sacco and Vanzetti and Tom Mooney. In the thirties the birth of industrial unionism was branded as being dominated by "reds"; so was the infant civil rights movement. President Bush leveled charges of "red" sympathies at Bill Clinton because he took part in Vietnam war protests and made a trip to the Soviet Union. But the post–World War II "anti-red" campaign was launched by Winston Churchill in Fulton, Missouri, when he said that an iron curtain had descended on Eastern Europe, thus giving rise to the Cold War.

But what was unique about the red scare of the fifties was the way in which the accusation of Communist could be directed against the most insignificant individuals, whether valid or not. Many lives in Hollywood were ruined, but it happened to figures of national importance as well—in government, in the press, and in universities, and some of those attacked have spent a lifetime trying to prove the groundlessness of the charges against them. Alger Hiss, for example. The man who prosecuted him was Richard Nixon and he became president. The man who fingered Hiss—Whittaker Chambers—was posthumously awarded the nation's highest civilian honor, the National Medal of Freedom, by President Reagan in 1984. Chambers was eulogized by William Buckley as the man who "reified the hard spiritual case against communism more successfully than any one of his generation." He certainly had his impact on Reagan, whose phrase "the evil empire," is right out of Chambers's book, *Witness*.

But why was the entertainment industry made such an important target? There were two reasons for congressional attacks: One was the potential for publicity. Movie stars commanded headlines. When Martin Dies, a Texas congressman who headed the HUAC in 1939, issued a subpoena for twelve-year-old Shirley Temple, it was big news—and laughable. It turned out that her press agent had sent a telegram in her name congratulating the French Communist Party for an election victory during the period of the Popular Front.

The other reason for congressional interest was an attempt at in-

* —PRICKS

timidation and thought control. Opposition to Hollywood began in the late thirties, in part because of certain films with social content such as *Juarez, Grapes Of Wrath, Blockade,* and *Confessions Of A Nazi Spy.* It grew with the militancy of Hollywood unions and the willingness of many movie celebrities to lend their names to progressive causes, including, in California at least, the Democratic Party, where for the first time in history a representative of that party—Culbert Olsen—was elected governor in 1938.

Unfortunately, there were superpatriots in Hollywood itself who had formed an organization called the Motion Picture Alliance for the Preservation of American Ideals. To what should be their everlasting shame, it is said that they provided spurious information to agents of HUAC and suggested the major investigation that began in 1947. Certainly, they were among the principal witnesses at the hearing who were making charges of Communist infiltration of the industry.

The "patriots" group was made up of actors, directors, and writers who had originally fought the unionization of their crafts on the grounds that they were artists and not workers. They then opposed the introduction of all political issues in union affairs, which was, in essence, a rather strong political stance in itself. Its chief ideologue was Ayn Rand, author of *The Fountainhead.* She wrote a guide of do's and don'ts for moviemakers which was widely circulated. "Don't smear the free enterprise system . . . Don't deify the common man . . . Don't make fun of success," and so forth.

The well-publicized formal HUAC hearings took place in October 1947 under the chairmanship of J. Parnell Thomas of New Jersey, who was later convicted of payroll padding and served his sentence in Danbury Federal Penitentiary alongside two of the unfriendly Hollywood Ten witnesses who had been convicted of contempt by his committee.

Representatives of the industry expressed a willingness to cooperate with the investigation but vehemently denied that any Communist propaganda appeared in their movies. Their lawyers were distinguished political figures such as Paul McNutt, who had been governor of the Phillipines, and James Byrnes, former secretary of state. Both stressed the patriotism of the industry and questioned the right of government agencies to tell the industry whom they could employ or what subjects were suitable for filming. Nevertheless it was a circus.

Many leading artists came to Washington to protest the government intimidation of the arts and artists—very much as they have in recent years, to oppose the curtailment of funds for the NEA because of its support of controversial artists. In 1947, a Committee for the First Amendment was formed, and a group of celebrities flew to Washington to protest the committee's actions. Here is a quote from a statement by Humphrey Bogart, undoubtedly written for him, which was used on the air waves:

> This is Humphrey Bogart. We sat in the committee room and heard it happening. We saw it happening. We said to ourselves it can happen here. We saw citizens denied the right to speak by elected representatives of the people. We saw police take citizens from the stand like criminals after they had been refused the right to defend themselves. We saw the gavel of the committee chairman cutting off the words of free Americans. The sound of that gavel, Mr. Thomas [the chairman], rings across America because every time your gavel struck it hit the First Amendment of the Constitution of the United States.

The refusal of the unfriendly witnesses to answer questions was based on a defense of their First Amendment right to freedom of speech, religion, and political belief. Their blatant hostility to the questioning, on the other hand, seemed to weaken their support. The attitude of director John Huston, a founder of the Committee for the First Amendment, was indicative of what would happen. He deplored the unconstitutional infringement on free speech by the House Un-American Activities Committee, but he was also turned off by the behavior of its victims. When the hearings adjourned, with the unfriendly witnesses cited for contempt, Thomas advised the industry representatives to set about immediately to "clean its own house and not wait for public opinion to force it to do so."

Hollywood hated this kind of publicity. A month later in a meeting of the heads of the major studios at the Waldorf-Astoria in New York City, the industry proclaimed its innocence of harboring subversives but swore to rid itself in the future of any possibility of "red" infection. Thus began, albeit reluctantly, the Hollywood blacklist. The first victims who were fired—if they were then employed—were the ten unfriendly witnesses.

A few who had contracts sued the studios and won, but the verdicts were thrown out by appellate courts, which sent the cases back for retrial. The retrials ended in out-of-court settlements for negligible sums, at least half of which went to the lawyers. The major case before federal courts—ultimately before the Supreme Court—to set aside the congressional contempt citations ultimately failed. (This was unexpected and probably due to the untimely deaths of two liberal justices, Frank Murphy and Wiley Rutledge, who might have tipped the balance in favor of the Hollywood Ten.)

I had thought the situation might blow over in a year or two—and perhaps it could have had the Ten won their decision in the courts. As it turned out, the blacklist situation got worse and I never went back to California. The investigating committee waited for the disposition of the Hollywood Ten case before calling additional witnesses, and they made it clear that they wanted more than a housecleaning of employed "reds." The industry had demonstrated that it could make films to influence public opinion. Why not films to alert people to the dangers of communism?

Movie moguls had always been nervous nellies when it came to outside pressure. They had caved in to the Catholic Legion of Decency in the early thirties and adopted the stringent motion picture production code. Part of this submissiveness was due to the fact that most of them were Jewish, immigrants, or children of immigrants who still marveled at and felt insecure with their wealth and importance in what was then described as the fourth-largest American industry. They were exceedingly vulnerable at the end of the forties: Their business was threatened by the antitrust order to divorce production from theater holdings and by the emergence of television.

So, beginning in 1950, at least a dozen films were made with blatant anti-Communist themes. Not one was a box-office success. In *Big Jim McLain,* made by Warners in 1952, John Wayne is actually an agent for the House Un-American Activities Committee. In the opening scene, when a college professor refuses to answer the committee's questions on the grounds of the Fifth Amendment, Wayne, as narrator, says:

> Eleven months. Eleven frustrating months. We rang doorbells and shuffled through a million feet of dull documents to prove to any intelligent person that these people were Communists, agents of the Kremlin—and they all walked out free. My fellow investigator—Mel Baxter—he hates these people. They had shot at him in Korea . . . The good doctor Carter could go right back to his well-paid chair as professor of economics at the University to contaminate more kids.

One film was actually called *The Red Menace* and another, *I Was a Communist for the FBI,* based on an allegedly true story about undercover agent Frank Cvetic, became the basis for a TV series.

The best known of these "anti-red" subjects was *My Son John*—possibly because it was directed by one of Hollywood's most successful directors, Leo McCarey, and featured the exalted queen of the theater, Helen Hayes, who had not made a film in seventeen years. In this movie, Helen's son, played by Robert Walker, has been a member of the Communist Party and is murdered by one of its agents. The movie ends with his tape recorded voice issuing a warning to the youth of America:

> Even now the eyes of Soviet agents are on some of you. Before I realized the enormity of the steps I had taken, I was an enemy of my country and a servant of a foreign power. I am a living lie, I am a traitor, I am a native American. Communist. Spy. And may God have mercy on my soul.

These Red-phobic subjects represented but a small percentage of the films turned out by Hollywood in the fifties, but the committee pressure had its effect. Not because a few leading artists were denied the opportunity to work but because socially critical subject matter became taboo. This happened in other areas as well. The personnel in other media—the radio, TV, and the press—as well as educators, publishers, and government employees, were subject to attack if they could be fingered as being affiliated with any organization identified on the attorney general's list as subversive.

These people could purge themselves by renouncing past affiliations, by demonstrating a change of heart, and by agreeing to cooperate in the campaign to root out subversives, which, in most instances, meant giving names of others who might be suspect. Or you could swear that you were not now and never had been and if you had joined a committee or signed a petition, you were duped. One important film and TV actress, Marsha Hunt, who had never been a Communist, was threatened with losing her job because a watchdog publication known as *Red Channels* called attention to her activities in antifascist organizations ten or more years earlier. She refused to say she was sorry, but offered to say, "If any of these activities furthered the cause of Communism, I regret having done them." This wasn't good enough, and the sponsor of her program replaced her.

Blacklisting certainly affected people—the victims, of course, but also those who took their jobs and felt some guilt about it, or those producers who could now hire outstanding writers to work without credit at one-third their former salaries. Blacklisted actors and direc-tors, however, were unemployable. Some gave up the profession al-together; some moved to other countries where they could work and where some had very successful careers, notably Joseph Losey (*The Servant* and *Accident*) and Jules Dassin (*Never On Sunday* and *Rififi*).

The impact of the blacklist on movie content, however, came from the industry's acceptance of outside influence to clean house, not only in terms of people but in terms of the issues to be presented on the screen. The result was that studios censored themselves where semi-political questions or matters of social content were involved. Jack Warner cut the lines, "*Your* father is a banker and *my* father lives over a grocery store," which were spoken by the poor John Garfield to the wealthy Joan Crawford in *Humoresque,* thus avoiding a reference to class conflict and pleasing conservative writer Ayn Rand, whose guidebook decreed we should not smear the free enterprise system. In John Huston's script for *The Treasure Of The Sierra Madre,* the old prospector, Walter Huston, says of some desperate Mexican bandits: "If our people lived in poverty under all sorts of tyrannies for hundreds of years back, we wouldn't know much about mercy either." But the line is cut from the Warner Bros. movie.

Social problems simply disappeared from the screen. Unwed mothers, tramps, prisoners who want to go straight, the plight of ten-ant farmers, injustices of all kinds were ignored. The films of the fifties protected the national image—ours was a splendid society and we were urged to cooperate with it, not to criticize.

But it's hard to make films without any problems at all—where's the conflict that makes a story? Well, there were musicals, of course. And three of the ten Academy Award–winners of the fifties were mu-sicals or closely related thereto—*An American in Paris, Around the World in Eighty Days,* and *Gigi.* Two were closely linked to show busi-ness—*All About Eve* and *The Greatest Show on Earth.* Then there were biblical epics where rebels are sanctified by their faith in God. So we had *Samson and Delilah, The Ten Commandments, Quo Vadis,* and *Ben Hur.* Director Cecil B. DeMille appears in a prologue to *The Ten Commandments* (a remake of his 1923 version) to say: "The theme of this picture is whether men are to be ruled by God's law or whether they are to be ruled by the whims of a dictator . . . This same battle continues throughout the world today." Previously, DeMille had clashed with Joseph Mankiewicz in the Directors Guild over the introduction of an anti-Communist oath and he resigned from that organization when, at first, they refused to adopt it.

One of the best films—an Academy Award–winner in 1955—was *On the Waterfront.* The movie is often construed as a glorification of informers since it was made by two talented people—Budd Schulberg and Elia Kazan—who had chosen to give names to the committee in order to continue working. Schulberg is my oldest friend and former Dartmouth roommate. In 1947, he was one of those who lent his name to attacks on the House Un-American Activities Committee, but in 1951 he was a cooperative witness, gave names, and gave in to the committee's demand that he endorse what they were doing. We had been friends since 1925, but we did not talk to each other for twelve years after his testimony. Such were the consequences of the witch hunt.

Actually, it was a simplistic but exciting movie, made in 1958, that marked a significant breakthrough from what must be characterized as the timid years of the fifties. The movie was *The Defiant Ones,* produced and directed by Stanley Kramer. The premise was that a black man (Sidney Poitier) and a white man (Tony Curtis), who hate each other because of ingrained racial prejudice, escape from a chain gang handcuffed to each other and learn that the only way they can survive is to cooperate with each other. One of the writers, Ned Young, had been an unfriendly witness before the HUAC in 1953 and, blacklisted, was forced to use the nom de plume of "Nathan Douglas" in his collaboration with Hal Smith. Their screenplay won an Academy Award, and it became known that blacklisted Ned Young was one of the authors. Nonetheless, his own name did not appear on a screen until 1968, three months after he died, as the author of an antifascist movie produced by my brother Matthew for Screen Gems and ABC. It was called *Shadows on the Land.*

The official movie industry blacklist was finally broken in 1960 when director Otto Preminger announced to the press that his movie *Exodus* (based on the Leon Uris novel), was written by the blacklisted writer Dalton Trumbo. By the mid-sixties, the atmosphere of fear gave way to new and bolder themes with *Dr. Strangelove, Bonnie and Clyde, Fail-Safe, Easy Rider,* and *M*A*S*H,* films with strong social content.

The story of the blacklist in the entertainment industry has often been told in print and in film and TV documentaries. But there are, so far as I know, only three feature length movies that have dealt with the subject—*The Front, The Way We Were,* and *Guilty by Suspicion.*

The best is the Walter Bernstein–Martin Ritt film, *The Front,* in which Woody Allen plays an idiot bookie who helps his TV writer friends by letting them use his name to sell their scripts. When ultimately called by the committee, he tells the HUAC group to go (bleep) themselves, for which he receives a jail sentence. The problem with *Guilty by Suspicion,* despite its good intentions, is that Robert De Niro, as the writer accused of Communist ties, is really innocent of the charge.

I was obviously not innocent of the charge, but how did I survive the blacklist?

Chapter 14

Postwar Problems and Sponsored Films

What happened in the movie field after the peace that ended World War II was in some ways extraordinary. So many writers, directors, and actors had participated in the struggle against the Axis powers that they were bound to return to Hollywood with a new perspective on their own work. Having once lived in the isolation of the Hollywood community, they now had an expanded vision. Many were determined that they would in the future work on movies that would reflect global problems, on useful entertainment subjects, and not necessarily on documentaries.

What they wanted to do was to propagate the ideals for which the war was fought—peace, justice, freedom from want, and an end to racial discrimination through equal opportunity for all. It was an extension of what FDR had spoken of as the four freedoms, and even some of the major producers proclaimed the need for a commitment to dramatize social themes.

My old boss, Darryl Zanuck, a Signal Corps colonel during the war, said, "We've got to move into new ground, break new trails. In short, we must play our part in the solution of the problems that torture the world." He was then preparing for Fox a movie biography of Woodrow Wilson and that president's fight for U.S. entry into the League of Nations—and an adaptation of Wendell Willkie's *One World*. But he qualified his commitment: "These pictures have something important to say, but they cannot say it unless people see them. I can tell you that unless these pictures are successful from every standpoint, I'll never make another film without Betty Grable in the cast."

Unfortunately, *Wilson* bombed and *One World* was never made.

But Zanuck's 20th Century–Fox studio did make *Pinky* and *Lost Boundaries* (which dealt with discrimination against blacks) and *Gentlemen's Agreement* (on anti-Semitism). During this postwar period other studios made *Crossfire, The Best Years of Our Lives, All the King's Men,* and *Home of the Brave,* all movies of social significance. Charlie Chaplin—who had attacked Hitler and fascism before the war with *The Great Dictator*—made a mordant comedy, *Monsieur Verdoux.* In the final scene, Chaplin, a modern Bluebeard, jailed for the murder of half a dozen wealthy women whom he has married for their money, expiates himself by saying how insignificant his crimes are compared to the mass murder of millions by the respectable makers of munitions.

All of these attempts to deal with social subjects—against war, racial or religious discrimination, and political corruption—were nipped in the bud because of the attack on the movie industry by super patriots of the extreme right wing. (American Legionnaires picketed *Monsieur Verdoux* so successfully that it was withdrawn from U.S. distribution after a few weeks.) And it was movies like these— plus some of the pro-Russian movies made during the war when the Soviets were our allies—that came under sharp attack when the House Un-American Activities Committee began its intensive attack on the industry in 1947.

Barred from work in the movie industry, I thought that there might be a place for me in the infant TV field. I had a lot of friends from college who were big shots in advertising agencies in New York. I thought that, with my Disney animation experience, I could at least write commercials. I went to see some of these old friends and made the mistake of answering, not the $64 question, but an equally devastating one: "Why did you leave Hollywood?" Answering that question honestly made my employment impossible. Subsequently I learned to clam up, to blame the move on ennui or the weather. But I burned a lot of bridges before I learned how to cross the river safely.

One New York TV producer was ready to give me an assignment until I decided that, because he was really a close friend, I ought to tell him that I was on the blacklist. When I did, he slammed his fist on the desk and said, "Why did you have to tell me? Don't you think I knew? Now I can't give you the job. Because if you got into trouble and they asked me why I hired you, I could have said that I didn't know. Now I can't."

Once I learned the lesson about keeping my mouth shut about my past, I found occasional work: a couple of screenplays without credit, some TV assignments calling for the use of phony names; but it was working on sponsored films that saved my neck.

Although *every* film is sponsored in one way or another, the "sponsored film" is made to fulfill the specific needs of the sponsor. It is the sponsor's brainchild and pet project. Although I was unemployable in Hollywood, I was acceptable as a writer for a variety of genuinely capitalist employers, including publishers, banks, steel companies, truck and auto makers, grocery chains, and even a few respectable eleemosynary groups such as the American Committee to Improve Our Neighborhoods, the American Cancer Society, and the International Rural Reconstruction Movement.

There are (or were) far more nonfiction movies than entertainment movies. Some of these appear on public broadcasting and the Discovery Channel. Some make it to the theaters (the old Cousteau films, *Woodstock, Roger and Me, The Thin Blue Line,* and *Hoop Dreams,* to name a few). But the vast number of nonfiction films are made for educational purposes—for sales, recruiting, and information—and are seen by very few people. (One friend did a fifty-thousand-dollar film for Martin-Marietta that was shown to five purchasing people in the Pentagon.)

I might very well have become a documentary filmmaker right after college if those left-wingers I had wanted to work with had been more receptive to my job search. The thirties, after all, were troublesome times, marked by worldwide depression and the growth of fascism. Many artists whom I admired—some of whom had used movies for personal expression—suddenly began to substitute social purpose for aesthetic experiment.

I met some of these people in the spring of 1935, my senior year at Dartmouth. I was a young radical, eager for a congenial career in theater or movies and—like most of my students today, but with far dimmer prospects—I was looking for a job. Someone had told me about a group being organized in New York to produce independent films of social significance. That sounded good to me, so it was to a loft on West 17th Street that I went to offer my services and there was introduced to photographer Ralph Steiner (a Dartmouth graduate) and some of his cronies who, as I recall, were either cooking up or putting the finishing touches to a short film called *Pie in the Sky* (which is still available from the Museum of Modern Art).

The visual credits to that picture, by the way, provide a nice piece of nostalgia. We see the photographer, Ralph Steiner, cranking away at his camera; the editor, Irving Lerner, at an editing table; the director, Molly Day Thatcher, and each of the leading actors, including Elia (Gadget) Kazan, later to be a famous director of stage and screen. The title is derived from the justifiably cynical lyrics of a well-known working class song, "You'll get pie in the sky by and by" and follows two unemployed guys who are on the tail end of a breadline at a mission and get nothing to eat. They hie themselves to the city dump where, despite being hungry, they pretend to be plutocrats, using the flotsam and jetsam items cast off by denizens of a busy metropolis. I guess it is the only film of Steiner's I've ever seen that had a sort of plot, but its social comment is handled with exuberance and wit.

My objective in 1935 was to edge my way into some of the action with this group, then known as the Film and Photo League, but I didn't succeed and wouldn't have had a paying job if I had. They were all professionals—most of them working at other jobs and making these noncommercial films as a sideline to explore the potentials of the medium and to fulfill a socially conscious commitment at the same time. Kazan worked as an actor with the Group Theater; Strand and Steiner did magazine photography; Herbert Kline was editing *New Theater* magazine; and Irving Lerner was working as an editor on short subjects for a major studio.

My actual career in sponsored films started in 1951 when I got a call from a talented artist, Abe Liss, who was establishing a New York office for the upstart West Coast animation company known as United Productions of America (UPA). I had written one film for them six years earlier when UPA was just getting started with refugees from the strike at Walt Disney's studio. The movie was *Brotherhood of Man*, a short animated subject that was based on a public affairs pamphlet by Columbia University anthropologists Ruth Benedict and Gene Weltfish and was sponsored in its screen version by the UAW/CIO.

In 1951 I hadn't had a paying writing job in three years, and I went to the UPA offices in New York with great eagerness. Liss had two projects that needed writers. And another writer was there whom I knew from Hollywood where he had been president of the Radio Writers Guild. His name was Sam Moore and he was also on the blacklist.

One project sounded like fun—it would be the first of a series of entertainment shorts dealing with family relations. The second one sounded like a formidable challenge—a promotional film for a lob-bying group known as "The Fragrance Foundation." In effect, it was a generic perfume commercial, featuring no brands but to be about ten minutes in length. What we didn't know at that point was which of us would do what, and Liss, a darling man, proposed flipping a coin. We decided instead to do both projects together, and thus be-gan a long-term collaboration that lasted almost thirty years.

The family film got made, by the way. It was called *Spare the Child.* Its premise was that a child switches places with his unreasonable fa-ther for a day and the father learns what it's like to be victimized by an abusive parent. We worked on the sponsored perfume promo for almost three months, actually getting as far as having an artist pre-pare an elaborate storyboard. But, in the long run, it was decided that goofy cartoon figures and the lofty essence of fragrance made strange bedfellows.

So I was working again but no longer writing screenplays for the-atrical films, and Sam was not writing nationally broadcast comedy shows (he and John Whedon had been responsible for *The Great Gildersleeve*). Nevertheless we had found a new outlet for our creative energies, and there were employers in New York who were willing to overlook the blacklist in order to get competent writers at bargain prices.

We did some black market television together, we wrote an occa-sional prospectus for a magazine or a new company, we even wrote some original stories for possible sale to the movies—under fictitious names, of course. For the most part, however, we preferred to work for pay, and that meant working on sponsored films. As professional writers, we were willing to write on any subject. If a potential em-ployer asked what our specialty was, we would simply ask what he needed. If it was a film on city planning, we were experts on city plan-ning; if it was medical, we were medical experts. Our philosophy—one that I have carried through life (and I think I learned it from Sam)—was that if you are a writer, you can write anything. And an-other important lesson, learned early on—never say you're not avail-able, even if you are already involved in ten other projects. Only one out of ten will come to fruition anyway.

What you do learn doing sponsored films is a lot about everything. Each assignment opens a new can of beans, introduces you to new people, to new problems, and frequently to new parts of the country or the world. (I went completely around the world twice.) We entered nooks and crannies of the business and industrial community that we never would have seen if we had stayed in show business. We learned about banking, the stock exchange, and computers before they became household items. We met presidents of major corporations and talked to auto workers on the assembly line in Detroit, to men stoking steel-making blast furnaces in Middletown, Ohio. We got used to the smell of linseed oil in a linoleum factory in Lancaster, Pennsylvania. Almost every assignment was a new learning experience, whether it was to find out what makes things tick at the Indianapolis 500 or how to teach safe driving to high school students. We didn't do films inimical to our beliefs, however. We never accepted an assignment to recruit for the armed services, although one of our film companies did a lot of military films for the government.

To be perfectly frank, my first job after the perfume fiasco resulted from turning down a possible assignment—an animated cartoon for the Continental Can Company, extolling the virtues of beer in cans. God knows I needed the job, but I also had an intense dislike for beer in cans—and still do. I amazed the animation director (Jack Zander, who eventually became one of my best friends) when I told him why I couldn't write the film, but he called me back the next day to offer me another assignment—an animated promotional film for Time Incorporated about the rosy prospects for the economy in the decade ahead (*The Changing American Market*). Even though I disagreed with the optimistic message, I accepted the assignment (and asked to work with Sam Moore) because I knew the film would be shown only to *Time*'s advertisers, one of the many "cheer up" messages I would write in years to come to loosen pocketbooks—in this case, those of advertisers.

Most of the films I did in the sponsored field I wrote with Sam Moore, but we occasionally took jobs separately and I actually started to direct the films I wrote, beginning in 1959. That, too, was something of a fluke. I had written the script for a film based on an article in *Fortune* magazine called *The Computer Comes to Marketing*. (This is 1959 and the computer is a huge piece of expensive equipment not in general use.) The film was to be sponsored by an accounting firm that hoped to attract clients with their computer expertise.

The script I wrote required actors, sets, and many of the accoutrements of a feature film, although the plot was simple: The top executives of a nameless company (I think they manufactured something called "Preebles") meet to decide whether or not to install a computer system, then travel around the country to locations where the equipment is already in use to determine whether they want to make the investment. The group's opinion is split, so they argue the pros and cons of computer use wherever they go—on a fishing boat, in a gym, in a bar, even in milady's chamber. It was a pretty complicated subject for a sponsored film and I wasn't sure we could find anyone in our field to direct it. "Sure, we can," said that sagacious and wonderful producer Walter Lowendahl. "Who?" "You," he said, and I became a director.

Now, I thought I knew something about making movies, but I found that I knew very little. Most of what I now know I learned during my years of directing sponsored films. For one thing, the sponsored film—while not a one-man show—is made with a very limited crew. If you direct and supervise the editing, as well as write the proposal and the original prospectus for shooting, you get for the most part what you have in mind and the only modifications come from the sponsors, who, if handled with care, can be more of a help than a hindrance.

You always tell sponsors that they know their business and you know yours. You won't tell them how to run their business and they shouldn't tell you how to run yours. But first, you must find out what they want. And that is not always easy. The president of a steel company may tell you that he just wants to present a favorable image of his company, but he usually thinks he should be put on camera to introduce it. But, you ask, why is he making a movie about it? There must be some problem he wants the movie to overcome. If there's no problem, why spend money on a movie? Ultimately, you find out that there *is* a problem.

In the case of a steel company like Armco, then of Middletown, Ohio, it was that everyone regarded steel companies as oldline, fuddy-duddy industries whereas, in fact, Armco considered itself a progressive, research-oriented company busily preparing for the twenty-first century. Knowing the problem, you begin to get an inkling of some possible conflict and drama.

I remember a similar situation with the Ford Motor Company. They wanted a film to show in high schools that would recruit graduates to work as auto mechanics in their dealerships. They wanted to explain about their splendid training programs, how the pay was much higher than if the same kids were to tote boxes in some supermarket, how they would get job security and a good chance for advancement—even to the point of having their own dealerships some day. It was such a rosy picture that I had to ask the old question, "Why make a movie? If you tell that story at a high school assembly, the kids should follow you like the pied piper to the nearest Ford dealer. What's the problem?"

Well, it turned out—as it usually does—that there *was* a problem. A lot of young guys didn't like the idea of being what they called "grease monkeys." To them, this meant having their fingernails coated with black grease and carrying the stigma of a dirty job when they wanted dates on Saturday nights. Find the reason for the sponsored film and maybe you can make it.

I even faced this problem in doing a recruiting film for Dartmouth College, which is, after all, a pretty nice place and one that a lot of kids would bust a gut to get into. I always say that it's almost impossible to make an interesting nonfiction film about the best of all possible worlds. And a small liberal arts college like Dartmouth, located on an elm-shaded plateau in the Connecticut River Valley, comes pretty close to being one of those "bests." If you look hard enough, however, you can find problems. The college *is* isolated and for many it's a long way from home. It has a reputation for too much drinking, for discrimination against women and minorities, and for being "jock." By the time you compile the list, you'll have more problems than you want to present. But even if you deal with one, you can make a positive message more convincing than if there is no argument at all.

Making documentaries has been facilitated by the new video cameras with lenses that have excellent low light capabilities and, of course, shooting and recording on videotape provides an instant review of what has been shot and recorded. Still, I was brought up on film and will always prefer it to video, despite the latter's convenience. A projected image from film is still far superior to anything that we in this country can project from a videotape—although that is sure to change with the advent of High Definition Television. But there is something tactile to the handling of film and sound tracks that can never be equalled when one is dependent on some expert in a white shirt twirling knobs.

One young filmmaker (Barry Brown) visited Dartmouth in the late sixties to show the first feature he had ever directed—*The Way We Live Now.* He had transported this subject in the usual film cans in the rear of his automobile. As writer, director, cameraman and editor, he clearly felt he had made the movie with his own hands. "Like Michelangelo," he said. "What's in those cans is my work—just as a piece of sculpture was Michelangelo's." It was a pretentious comparison, but he meant it. The only thing he didn't do, he said, was to mix the sound and next time around, he said he'd do that, too. One student, while admiring Brown's effort said, "His do-it-yourself mania is a crock. It's like a novelist cutting down a tree with an axe he made so that he could manufacture his own pencils and paper before writing a novel."

Making movies is great fun. Orson Welles talked at one time about the joy of having the great Hollywood toy to play with. Well, the sponsored film field is a little like that. You can, with luck, find someone willing to pay for work with your favorite toy—even if you can't do subjects of your choice. And if you are a writer, you can always "moonlight"—as I did when I added the job of film critic to what I was already doing.

Chapter 15

How I Became a Critic

Getting a job as a movie critic in the late sixties was, like getting into sponsored films, due to a fluke. I was going to Montreal for the World's Fair—Expo 67—and needed a press pass to avoid hourlong waits for the popular exhibits featuring movies. I went to see an old friend, Dave Scherman (Dartmouth '36), an ace photographer who was then the editor of the front of the book section of *Life*, at that time a weekly magazine of pictures and text. He said he would give me a pass if I would write a seven-hundred-word piece about the movies I saw at Expo. When I turned it in, Scherman liked the piece, primarily because, while praising the new movie technology, it decried the absence of legitimate content. He then asked me to do one movie review a month to relieve their regular critic, Dick Schickel, who was writing a book, and I did this for three years.

A year later, another friend, Art Hettich, who had been the PR man for *Family Circle* and for whom I had written and directed a couple of promotional films, became the publisher of that magazine. He was a movie buff and asked if I would write a monthly page of movie reviews for him. I cleared this with Scherman at *Life* who saw no conflict of interest but wondered how I could adjust my viewpoint to satisfy the needs of two entirely different readerships.

Life was a mass magazine but the front of the book—with its literary, music, and art pieces—clearly appealed to a sophisticated audience, while *Family Circle* derived all of its circulation from sales at supermarket checkout counters. Since I would write about only one or two movies a month for each magazine, I intended to write primarily about movies I liked and I thought I could choose movies for each magazine that would appeal to its particular readers. For the most part, it worked, though occasionally, as in the case of *2001* and *Shoes of the Fishermen,* I had to write about the same movie for two different audiences.

Writing monthly, I was often forced to review movies that had been thoroughly chewed over by other critics, so I tried, as often as possible, to incorporate a general theme about movies in each of the pieces. For example, in writing about Marlon Brando's role in a run-of-the-mill film like *Morituri,* I took off on the subject of the reluctant hero; about Marco Bellochio's *Fist in His Pocket,* on the subject of first-time directors frequently making a big splash and then never repeating the success; about *Yours, Mine and Ours,* how skilled, mature performers like Lucille Ball and Henry Fonda could convince you that they had a good time in bed without ever showing it. (The gimmick in that movie is that when they marry, each widowed, they have a combined family of eighteen children and Lucille gets pregnant again.)

It seems hard to believe, but in order to write about maybe two dozen movies a year I had to see practically every movie that was released. I went to movies almost every day, and at year's end when I got my Guild ballots to vote for awards, I found ~~that~~ I had seen nearly two hundred movies. In 1996—with no responsibilities as a critic—I saw twenty new releases.

Because today's critics are overwhelmed with screenings and receive hefty printed handouts of information about each movie they see (including lengthy synopses and biographies of everyone connected with the venture, sometimes even including the hairdresser), they are naturally eager to "like" something and, after suffering through a batch of "dogs," they may go off half-cocked with praise about a movie that is merely mediocre. Certainly, the publicity departments of the major distributing companies, who are responsible for what they call "press screenings," work very hard to create a favorable reaction for every new feature they handle.

New York and Hollywood are the principal locales for the presentation of new works. Most of the major studios in Hollywood have their own projection rooms; some of the companies have screening rooms in their New York headquarters. Others rent screening rooms of various sizes, depending on the nature of the movie. They schedule a series of showings to accommodate the hundreds of people accredited as critics. These include the reps of the local press, national magazines, syndicates, and TV; all of the radio commentators and a lot of hangers-on with notebooks, cameras and assorted paraphernalia whose affiliations are questionable at best. Obviously, the company press agents and the freelance PR people who are hired by independents are primarily concerned about the critics from the major newspapers (Janet Maslin of the *New York Times*), national magazines (David Ansen of *Newsweek,* Richard Corliss of *Time*) and television (Siskel and Ebert).

Not that PR folk can buy a good review with a lunch at 21 or by providing an intimate interview with Michelle Pfeiffer in her suite at the Plaza, but such gestures help. Good movie critics are pretty incorruptible, but that doesn't prevent the press agents from trying. They have been known to preview new movies on Caribbean islands, providing transportation and a three-day holiday to a select few.

I learned about the racket of movie criticism during my years with *Life* and *Family Circle.* Universal Pictures made it a practice to serve hors d'oeuvres and drinks after screenings in their comfortable projection room at Fifty-Seventh Street and Park Avenue in New York. The room itself accommodated about forty. Once a Universal rep asked the forbidden question, "What did you think?" before I got on an elevator. I smiled and thanked him for the drinks but didn't answer.

On another occasion, in the Paramount screening room when it was on a top floor of the old Paramount Theater building in Times Square, I showed such obvious appreciation (a few tears, for one thing) for Zeffirelli's *Romeo and Juliet* that the press agent, knowing that I obviously had liked the movie, called the next day to ask if my magazine (*Life*) would consider running a review before the film opened (a practice that was usually frowned on by distributors). *Life* agreed and a quote from my review appeared in big letters for about a month on a Times Square billboard: "The most satisfactory film I've seen this year."

Life had a paid circulation of about eight million and was said to be seen—according to the "accumulated audience" theory—by about 26,000,000 people a week. Favorable quotes from *Life* reviews were therefore at a premium and were frequently quoted—often out of context. In addition, editors liked to have their magazine reviews quoted. When I made a scrupulous effort to avoid being quoted unless I really liked a film and tried to avoid hyperbolic words like "brilliant" or "scintillating," which could be used indiscriminately, I was told to loosen up.

I once wrote up a mediocre movie as an example of then current spy movies that made no sense. What I said in *Life* was the following:

Have you been worrying lately about the fact that you can't understand spy movies any more? That even while you are enjoying the hell
out of them, you feel a little guilty because you leave the theater totally
bewildered as to who won, or why? . . . *A Dandy in Aspic,* the newest
one, is a perfect case in point. Spies and counterspies hotfoot around
a Berlin which never looked lovelier. Actors—skillfully cast down to
the smallest role—provide exciting, clever scenes. The film has everything—but logic. There is no "message," or hardly any, and in its absence the fancy new medium has to carry the ball. In *A Dandy In Aspic,* it does so with gusto and skill.

What Columbia Pictures quoted in its ads was:

Done with gusto and skill. The plotting is the first of the enjoyment
bonuses, another is the proliferation of CRISP, CLEVER, EXCIT-
ING, BRILLIANT SCENES, skillfully cast down to its smallest role.

They had turned a tongue-in-cheek "pan" into an endorsement. I
wrote to the head PR man at Columbia to complain:

The implication is that I liked the plot when, in fact, the premise of
my review was that the plot made no sense at all. I also object to that
string of hyperbolic adjectives drawn arbitrarily from various parts of
the review—"crisp, clever, exciting, brilliant." No reviewer worth his
salt would ever include all those in one sentence and when you make
me sound illiterate you undermine my left-handed endorsement of
your film. I did say there were clever and exciting scenes. Elsewhere I
said they were "crisp." The word "brilliant" is taken completely out of
context."

They then revised the ad copy to say: "Done with gusto and skill! The
do-it-yourself plotting is the first of the enjoyment bonuses; another
is the proliferation of CRISP, CLEVER SCENES. Skillfully cast
down to the smallest role."

While we're commiserating with critics about their ordeals, did
you ever wonder how some of them manage to quote the lines from
a movie verbatim? I can provide a variety of answers. One is that
many critics have remarkable recall. Another is that some call the
press agents and ask for quotable excerpts from the screenplay. Today,
some are given videotapes that can be re-run for exact quotes. Some
use pocket tape recorders and turn them on from time to time to
show off how good their ears and memories are. Others take notes in

the dark. (I once sat next to <u>Pauline Kael</u> at a preview of Fellini's
Satyricon and had the impression that she never stopped writing.) Another method—which I used until I got too many complaints from
paying customers—was to take notes with a "light-up pen." One old-
timer pulled a 35-millimeter camera out of his shoulderbag, got a
focus on the screen, and could be heard clicking away repeatedly once
the lights went down. I saw him recently at a press screening of the
New York Film Festival, looking a lot older, but still carrying the same
shoulderbag, sitting down front in the 1,500 seat Alice Tully Hall,
and I am sure that when the lights went down he was still clicking.
What he did with the pictures, I never knew.

Professional critics, like the rest of us, have their pets and they will
bend over backwards to defend even the poorest work of the chosen.
Vincent Canby of the *Times* could find little fault or flaw with the
work of the late <u>François Truffaut,</u> and his consistent enthusiasm for
the works of <u>Woody Allen</u> have had a lot to do with establishing
Allen's esteemed reputation. Both Allen and Truffaut, however, are
"total" filmmakers. Unfortunately, some critics, as well as some film
scholars who consider themselves critics, are still addicted to the "au-
teur" theory (the cult of the director), and these auteurists often fail
to mention the writer or other talents who contribute significantly to
a finished film. And while it is true that directors with established
reputations—Kubrick, Scorcese, Altman, and so forth—deserve to
have each of their works evaluated with due regard for what they have
done in the past, they can fall on their faces, too, and the critic should
be willing to say so. The director's work is, after all, quite visible. The
writer's work can be judged only as it is presented by the director and
his cast. But the old truism that one cannot make a good picture with
a bad script, but one can surely make a bad picture from a good script,
still holds. It is not easy, however, for the critic to tell when this has
happened.

Vincent Canby is a friend of mine and one of the most informed
and effective movie critics in the business, but I often tell a writer versus director story at his expense. It has to do with the gala showing of
*M*A*S*H* at the Cannes Film Festival in 1970. Canby was there, as
was director Robert Altman, producer Ingo Preminger, actresses <u>Sally</u>
<u>Kellerman</u> and Jo Ann Pflug, and screenwriter <u>Ring Lardner Jr.</u> Ac-
cording to Lardner, everyone was photographed when Candice
Bergen handed out the Golden Palm Award at the Festival screening,
but when Canby—who liked the movie—described this auspicious

event in the *New York Times* he mentioned everyone but writer Lard-ner. Like most of the press—and the public, in the long run—Canby accepted Altman's claim that he barely used the script and ~~that~~ most of the dialogue as well as the action was ad-libbed on the set. Any reading of Lardner's screenplay will knock the director's conceit into a cocked hat. (But producing companies do not, as a rule, make screenplays available to reviewers.)

A year or so later, there came a film (*The Deadly Trap*) directed by a noted Frenchman, René Clement, that Canby correctly character-ized as a "turkey." In this case, however, instead of laying blame on the illustrious French director, he not only named the man who got screenplay credit for the fiasco (Sidney Buchman) but also named the other writers, including Ring Lardner, who had worked on the pro-ject without contributing enough to get any credit at all.

I have taught courses in practical film criticism. The primary ad-vantage of such courses is that students seem genuinely eager to prac-tice critical writing on a subject in which they are definitely inter-ested. The hardest thing to get students to do is to summarize succinctly what a movie is about and to avoid the tendency to gush or puke without giving the reason why. There are a few books on film criticism and quite a few anthologies of criticism by well-known crit-ics: Otis Ferguson, James Agee, Pauline Kael, Stanley Kaufman, Ju-dith Crist, and Richard Schickel, to name a few. There were, at one time, annual publications by the New York Society of Film Critics, which were interesting for the fact that they published differing views of the same movie. The best book of this sort was *Film As Film* by Boyum and Scott, which is now out of print. It gave the authors' views and then gave contrasting reviews of a series of well-known movies, both foreign and domestic.

But the big question, at all times, will always be, "What did you think?" And the answer to that question, still unresolved, has been the modus vivendi for my career as a teacher for the past thirty years.

Chapter 16

About Becoming a Film Studies Teacher

My teaching career began in 1966 when I got a call from an old friend, Professor Henry Williams, head of the Drama section of the English Department at Dartmouth.

The first postwar film course at Dartmouth was launched in 1964. The idea originated with Orton Hicks, then vice president of the college and a former film executive. Professor Williams, who always loved movies, got the Drama steering committee of the English Department to approve it, even drawing up a petition and inducing students to gather two hundred signatures outside of Thayer Hall (where the students ate their meals) to demonstrate support. The petition, however, didn't impress the Committee on Instruction, which had to approve for the Humanities Division. The committee thought, as Williams put it, "such a course hardly fitting since it was backed by no vast body of literature." To which Williams allegedly replied, "There is indeed a literature, not in books but in cans."

I should explain that movies had been held in low esteem by the upper classes and the intelligentsia from their inception. In the early days of the twentieth century, actors, in need of jobs and money, would sneak into movie studios looking for work and asking that their names be kept secret. It was actually the prestige of a husband-and-wife team, Mary Pickford and Douglas Fairbanks, that gave the movie industry a certain legitimacy. The result was that celebrities such as Lindbergh, G. B. Shaw, and President Coolidge insisted on touring the studios when they came to California. Louis B. Mayer was ultimately acknowledged as a supporter of Republican president Herbert Hoover, and it was rumored that if Hoover were re-elected in 1932, Mayer would be apppointed ambassador to Turkey.

At Dartmouth, the idea of movies as "canned literature" didn't impress the academic decision makers so Williams conspired to introduce the movie course anyway—as a *seminar* that required no division approval at all. And that's how Film Studies got into the curriculum.

That seminar was taught by a charming and knowledgable movie exhibitor, Arthur L. Mayer, Harvard '08, who had been "hired" for the job by vice president Hicks even before Henry's skulduggery made the job possible—a breach of academic protocol no one ever regretted. Although Mayer had no teaching experience and the department insisted that Williams monitor his performance, the vigilance proved unnecessary. Mayer's life spanned the entire history of the movies. He had known personally most of the film greats from D. W. Griffith to Fellini. He had been a press agent for the first sexy Mae West films, but he had also imported to the United States the first great classics of postwar Italian Neo-Realism. He represented the precise combination of art and commercialism that is the unique quality of the movies. He was an extraordinary raconteur, and his personal anecdotes about people and moviemaking—though sometimes apocryphal—both charmed and educated his students. The seminar was such a success that it was accepted without question as a regular course in the curriculum for the following year.

Because of his success at Dartmouth, Mayer began teaching year-round, adding Stanford and USC to his schedule. But he was almost eighty and necessarily talked of retirement. When he agreed to do "just one more year," Williams called me—I was writing and directing sponsored films in New York—and asked if I would be willing to take over. I was flattered but taken aback because although, like Arthur, I knew a lot about movies, I had never taught at all.

I agreed to spend a term in Hanover the following spring, presumably to observe Arthur Mayer's last class sessions. After the first week, I told Williams that I couldn't possibly fill the shoes of this remarkable man. And fortunately for the students at Dartmouth, I never had to. Mayer's "one more year" stretched to eleven and, as his potential replacement, I stood in the wings without a call until he finally did retire at the age of ninety-one.

In the meanwhile, however, Williams induced me to teach a course of my own having to do with theory, writing, and production which for better or worse, significantly altered the course of my life. It was about the same time that Drama moved out of English and became a department on its own. The two film courses went with it, the program ultimately expanding, with more courses for me and an added faculty member to become what is now the film studies department.

Film studies is now a recognized part of most college curricula, but it was a recognition not easily achieved. To this day, there are those who cannot conceive of the movies as an art form worthy of serious study. If one looks at the general output of commercial filmmakers, it is easy to understand this skepticism. After all, we are dealing with a commercial medium that is barely one hundred years old. And it started as nothing more than a technical novelty: moving pictures of the world around us, which, with a little manipulation (and a few actors) could be used to tell stories.

The academic respectability of movies had an auspicious beginning in October 1965, when a conference on "Film Study in Higher Education," sponsored by Dartmouth in association with the American Council on Education, was held in the new Hopkins Center complex, built to house the arts at the college.

Now regarded as a landmark in the film study movement, this conference brought together the nation's leading film educators, critics, historians, and a few professionals. It played a major role in stimulating the formation of the American Film Institute. The importance of movies in contemporary culture was clearly established but *how* or even *whether* it should be taught became a subject for entertaining, sometimes acrimonious, debate. As critic Pauline Kael—one of those who attended—put it, "If you think the movies can't be killed, you underestimate the power of education."

I must admit that, like Pauline, I was somewhat appalled by some of the esoteric language that was used to describe what I regarded as an accessible mass medium of entertainment. I wrote a piece that year for the *Directors Guild Magazine* that was reprinted in the *Dartmouth Alumni Magazine,* in which I said:

> When you attend a Conference on Film Study in Higher Education, as I did at Dartmouth College in 1965, and when you hear scholars discussing a variety of approaches to the study of film art, history, and technique, you're bound to be impressed, if not pleased. After all, this is your area of daily work and it is being clothed with academic dignity. But what happens to your chosen medium in the process? Well, here's the way one professor from a Midwest university described part of his course: "Discussion proceeds from cross generic contrast among documentary, fiction, and experimental films in terms of their as-

cending order of abstraction from reality as generally perceived." Now what do you suppose old-time movie directors like Woody Van Dyke or Mickey Neilan would have said to that?

After thirty years, I am still teaching (though I'm listed as Director Emeritus) and since Film Studies is now a department, I think it's safe to say that film studies has passed the trial stages and, despite critic Kael's dire prophecies—and my misgivings—we seem to have enhanced rather than killed the undergraduate's long-standing passion for the movies.

At Dartmouth we have consistently linked movies to the liberal arts curriculum. A good moviemaker or scholar should be something of a Renaissance person because the movies themselves embrace such a vast spectrum of the arts and crafts. Today, a student can major in film studies. Most are interested in production, a few in critical studies. But we emphasize the need for familiarity with drama and literature, with the visual arts, music, and languages as well as the social sciences. Dartmouth film students know that there's more to making an effective movie than turning the camera on the world around them and recording what they see. First comes the word and that means studying screenplays.

When the COI (Committee on Instruction) turned down a possible film course because of a lack of literature about the subject, they were essentially correct. But the number of books about the movies has increased a hundredfold since the mid-sixties. Every major publishing house has gotten into the act. Each is pushing its own big, illustrated film history book. There are hundreds of biographies. Books about every period, every genre, about documentaries, about animation, and dozens of books about production, not only of film but of television.

For someone like me, who entered the movies because it was the family business, all of this academic attention is both satisfying and alarming. I am appalled at the number of students who choose this risky business for their lifework. Multiply our little undergraduate program at Dartmouth by the hundreds of film study programs that now exist across the country, then consider the output of about forty graduate film programs, and you know how stiff the competition for jobs is going to be. Quite frankly, I urge even the most promising students—if their parents can afford to send them to graduate school—to get an M.B.A. or a law degree or some entitlement certificate that guarantees a substantial living. Then, after they make their first million, borrow a little more and make a movie. But start at the top.

If that sage advice doesn't work, I can only urge them to use screenwriting as a passport to the industry. One can write scripts while working behind a bar or in a supermarket. It may take forever and the odds are long, but you don't need a camera, an editing room, or a whole studio to write a script.

And for those colleges and universities that have no film study programs at all, it should be clear that film society programs can provide a thorough extracurricular education in film culture. Consider how much a student can learn if he is exposed to one or two film classics a week over a four-year period. A film society was the only source of movie education at Dartmouth in the early fifties, but that period produced writers Buck Henry and Steve Kandel, directors Bob Rafelson and Jim Goldstone, and producers David Picker, Don Hyatt, and Bud de Rochemont.

Chapter 17

In Conclusion

This is not a book about the making or appreciation of movies, although I would hope it might offer some ideas to those involved in both activities. I have, in the course of thirty years, taught a variety of classes in production and writing—for both film and video, in history, in theory, in specific genres like the documentary, and a variety of courses in practical and theoretical criticism. But in all of these courses, I have consistently emphasized the importance of the writer because without his or her contribution, the moviemaking process simply cannot take place.

There are actually five stages of film production—literary, administrative, production, editing, and marketing. But nothing happens until stage one is complete and a script is written. When, in these days of my retirement, I was told I could teach but one class, I had no difficulty making the choice. It would be "Writing for the Screen," and someday, somehow, someone from that class will write the superscript that changes the course of movie history.

In the meantime the best I can do is pass on to these talented young people some of the knowledge I have gleaned about the creative process and how to harness it for optimum results on the screen. One example of this, which is intended to overcome reticence about telling stories that are not entirely original, is a brief handout outlining the most familiar plots and premises I could think of. Here it is:

The success story: Horatio Alger, David and Goliath, Jack and the Beanstalk, Cinderella.

The prodigal son: The person who leaves family, home, sweetheart, and established values to live an easier and gayer life, usually with ruinous results, so that he or she returns much chastened.

The sacrifice plot: Whether of father, mother, brother, husband, sweetheart, or friend. It is done these days with more of an ironic touch in which the sacrifice proves to have been in vain—as in *Mildred Pierce. Stella Dallas* is a classic example.

The love plot: Not necessarily between the sexes, which is usually outlined by boy meets girl, boy loses girl, boy gets girl. It can be a mother or father for a child, brothers, friends, and so forth.

The triangle: The most familiar way to work with the love plot—involving two men and a woman, or two women and a man or combinations thereof. As in 1993's *Age of Innocence.*

Domestic relations: Problems of married life—parents and alienated children. *Kramer vs. Kramer, Terms of Endearment.*

Reformation of character: The hard guy who turns soft, the weakling who becomes tough, the crook who goes straight, the whore who performs a noble deed, and so forth.

And the opposite of the above.

The adventure plot: Usually involves a quest—rescuing someone in distress or recovering something of value like the Holy Grail or the Stepford files or the crown jewels. Can also be about achieving some seemingly unattainable goal, like reaching the North Pole or canoeing down the Colorado.

The heist plot: Variation of the adventure plot in which the objective is to pull off a major theft or scam.

The detection plot: Solving a crime.

The ideological conflict plot: Putting together two people with sharply divided views on politics, sex, religion, whatever. Like the relationship between the two FBI men in *Mississippi Burning.* Buddy cops, one who wants to kill the rascals, the other who wants to reform them.

Revenge plots: Based on settling a score, righting some wrong, a family feud. From *Hamlet* to *High Noon.*

Fantasy: Deals made with characters from heaven or hell, talismans or potions that give people unique powers—to fly, to become invisible, to predict the future, to live again. You name it.

Escape plots: Obvious, as illustrated by most prison flicks, *Grand Illusion, Stalag 17,* and so forth.

Grand Hotel plots: Group of people with various problems in a given locale. Often begins or ends with a disaster affecting everyone—as in a plane crash, earthquake, or fire.

Sci-fi plots: Desperate attempts by protagonists to combat threatening forces with superhuman power which are sometimes extraterrestrial.

Mistaken identity plots: Which can be used for either comedy or drama or both. *North by Northwest* is an example.

Stranger in the house plots: Used for comedy as in *The Man Who Came to Dinner* or for drama as in *The Lodger.*

Road plots: Someone has to or wants to go someplace and meets a variety of problems along the way, which may or may not alter the original goal.

What everyone should realize is that no matter how familiar the plot or premise may be, the important thing is how it is treated. How much freshness of character, of background—even of topicality—can be brought to it. And implicit in most plots is a goal of some kind for the principal character or characters—something that is desired or something to be avoided—and an opposing force, whether a person, an institution, or a natural phenomenon interfering with the objective. And in a lot of movies, the objectives shift as the story progresses.

Most of what I have written in this book pertains to movies made in the United States, with which I am most familiar, and most of my illustrations are from movies made by the Hollywood industry before 1970. That's because I was a more ardent moviegoer twenty-five years ago than I am today. Moviegoing was then my business, of course, but it was also pleasurable. In recent years, I have been eager to see only a handful of movies, and, almost without exception, they have been made far from Hollywood. I think of Ireland's *My Left Foot,* China's *Farewell My Concubine,* Australia's *Walkabout,* and American independent movies like *Boyz N the Hood* and *The Brothers McMullen.*

Can it be old age that clouds my view of current movies, that causes most of the new young leading ladies such as Wynona Ryder and Barbara Hershey and Debra Winger to look so much alike that I can't tell one from the other? Is it elderly prudishness that causes me to resent every scene in a bedroom which is shot from behind the heroine facing her man and dropping her dress and slip? I can certainly remember when we writers wished we could use an occasional "damn," but now that the restrictions are gone, is it necessary to use the word "fuck" a dozen times in a single scene?

I am something of a curmudgeon in thinking ~~that~~ we are currently in an explicit sex quagmire. I am not happy with violence, gore, and objectionable street language as elements ~~that are~~ used to titillate and attract audiences. When these elements are directed at what the industry perceives to be its primary audience—the group between sixteen and twenty-eight—and when it is assumed ~~that~~ an audience of popcorn gobblers and coke swizzlers will be bored with anything less than four-letter words, head-bashing, shootouts, gore, and the sighs, grunts, and exotic exercises of various sexes between the sheets, then the producers are not only underestimating the intelligence of their audience but doing a disservice to the fiber of American culture.

The death knell of the movies has been sounded in the past. The advent of sound was expected by many to put an end to the medium as an art form. The blacklist was expected to put an end to its creative potential for social comment and the advent of television would put an end to theater-going. The current trend of sex and violence could possibly reduce movies to the level of comic strips. But it won't. ?

I'M NOT SO SURE

APPENDIX A

Tributes to People I Loved and
from Whom I Learned

LOUISE SEIDEL RAPF

Louise Rapf, my beloved wife of fifty-four years, started work as a child model when she was six, went on the stage as an acrobatic tap and toe dancer at eleven, went to Hollywood with a Warner Bros. contract at sixteen and, as a result, never wanted to perform again after she got married. To her dying day, remembering her own exploitation as a youngster, she was revolted by the sight of child performers on screen or TV. She was probably the most astute movie critic I ever knew and cued most of my own reactions to movies with little more than a laugh or an exasperated sigh. Comments at graveside on April 11, 1993:

Because she was a strikingly beautiful tow-haired child, her parents were besieged with offers from model agencies and she appeared in dozens of print ads after World War I, an onerous experience that caused her in later years to rail loudly at the increasing use of cuddly moppets to sell everything from cereal to tires on commercial TV.

She did end up with a contract in Hollywood, which was lucky for me, for that is where we met.

Probably her favorite role was in Leo McCarey's *Make Way for Tomorrow* as the sympathetic hatcheck girl who shows respect and kindness to a pair of old people (Beulah Bondi and Victor Moore) who are having their last date before being shipped off by their children to separate nursing homes.

Louise's long and affectionate affair with Dartmouth College began when I made Winter Carnival one of the stops on our honeymoon. Later, with her Hollywood and show business background, she was not only a hostess and den mother to generations of Dartmouth Film Studies undergraduates, for whom she often did acting stints in films and videotapes, but she was also a role model and an inspiration.

She launched an intense educational career as a star auditor of college classes in the sixties, never cutting, and doing all the work in courses as diverse as Chaucer and geography. As the late Professor Henry Williams said after she (with Arthur Mayer's wife, Lillie) had completed his course in early American drama in 1969, "The presence of these two ladies proves that what this school needs is co-education." Two years later, Dartmouth got just that. . . .

For me our marriage was a long and wonderful trip—a script. A story. And like all stories, it had its moments of strong conflict, as well as those of love and reconciliation.

One young woman, enrolled in my screenwriting class last winter, wrote with amazing insight how impressed she was by our devotion to each other or—in her words—by "a long fifty years of love and bickering."

How could this student know that one of the last things Louise said to me in the hospital when I told her she could not get out of bed to go to the bathroom, "Husbands are not supposed to tell wives what to do"?

J. BLAIR WATSON

Watson became audiovisual director at Dartmouth College when he was released from the Air Force in 1946. Though he was never assigned officially as a teacher, he taught more Dartmouth undergraduates about movies than anyone else. Remarks at a memorial tribute to Watson in Hopkins Center on May 11, 1991:

He was a very private person. As well as I knew him, I have no idea where he stood politically except that he always lined up on the side of human decency. With all his accomplishments—and they were many—Blair was certainly not the model of an aggressive go-getter. He was strictly low-key and about the only thing that clearly riled him was sloppiness and disorder—both physical and mental. In the face of adversity, he had the patience of Job. He didn't get excited, he didn't get mad, and too much enthusiasm would simply embarrass him. He was a unique kind of leader, who usually gave the impression that he was being led.

The way he managed to start the Dartmouth Film Society is a good example. There is no way it could have come into being without his active support. And since I was there at the time, I can attest to the fact that it was something he very much wanted. He simply waited for the demand.

With Blair's office arranging the bookings, students actually started a series of Sunday afternoon screenings of documentaries, foreign films, and classics in 1948. Interest was there and the formal subscription series started with *All Quiet on the Western Front* and continued at two-week intervals at 9 P.M. concluding in April of 1949 with the Marx Brothers in *Duck Soup*. There were 325 subscribers. The cost: $3.50.

For years the membership fee stayed under five dollars and Blair was reluctant to raise it. In Blair's opinion, the Film Society, which moved to a 900-seat theater in the new arts complex, Hopkins Center, in 1962 was part of the center's commitment to the education of students and to the cultural stimulation of the community. As a good Scotsman Blair liked to show a profit, but as an educator he could easily rationalize a loss. And there were frequent losses to rationalize after academic film courses crept into the curriculum in the mid-sixties. The reason was that Blair urged the student film society directorates to support courses with useful screenings. This worked fine for Arthur Mayer's film history classes, but a heavy dose of Buñuel, Antonioni, or Godard in support of particular courses (and we had them) could put a series in the red. . . .

It is hard to imagine how he managed to cope with so many eager film buffs over so long a period of time, some from small towns who loved Frank Capra but had never heard of John Grierson or Pare Lorentz, others from urban centers who knew the works of André Wajda and Dusan Makavejev and wanted series dedicated to films of Eastern Europe. Somehow, he survived this pressure from the pretentious and the naive and managed to teach his charges how to keep the organization going; how to meet deadlines for programming, printing, promoting, selling tickets, handling admission, ushering, and, occasionally, even how to put together a film society baseball team that could beat nine students from the *Daily Dartmouth*.

That was Blair. A remarkable man, unique and irreplaceable. He never really forgot a student. And we will never forget him.

SAM MOORE

Moore was a radio writer, president of Radio Writers Guild, blacklisted in 1951, and my collaborator on various projects, predominantly sponsored films, from 1951 to 1980. Remarks at a memorial service for Sam in my New York apartment on December 17, 1989:

In 1932, seven years out of college, he got a job as a reporter on the old *New York Herald Tribune* under editor Stanley Walker—a prestigious spot for any writer in those days—and accordingly underpaid. He'd been there six months when, through a friend, he was offered a job writing radio at the J. Walter Thompson Agency for three times the money he was being paid at the *Herald Trib.* As Sam later wrote in an incomplete memoir, *Me and Radio,* "I did not own a radio. I had never listened to a radio program, but I had a wife and two children and I snapped at the offer." As he was to say so often in the future, "A writer can write anything."

Sam learned the radio-writing business at the agency, writing commercials and contributing occasional sketches to the big shows. In his memoir, Sam recalls the first sketch he ever wrote. It was for Georgie Jessel who was filling in on the *Sunday Night Eddie Cantor Show.* The boss called him in on Monday and told him it played great. "So there it was," he wrote, "My sketch played for an audience of millions, had the studio audience in stitches, and I hadn't even heard it. That day I bought a radio. . . ." Sam was, in fact, a master of the hard sell—something he must have learned in his novice days with the J. Walter Thompson advertising agency. And a lot of the stuff we wrote as a team had to end up with a hard sell—why advertising in *Life* magazine paid off, why every good citizen should be concerned to clean up his neighborhood, why taking vitamins could save your health and maybe even bring you luck. Sam could write those speeches with force and persuasion and, since we often worked with animated characters, the speeches were delivered by elephants, bears, owls, and other funny-looking creatures from Noah's ark who, once anthropomorphized, could put a sugar coating on the sponsor's message. . . .

It was the blacklist that brought us together in 1952. He was probably out of work. I know I was. We met in the New York offices of UPA, vying for the better of two assignments. We decided to do both in collaboration and continued to collaborate for the next thirty years, at the end of which time, both well along in years, we were still known as "the boys". . . .

I passed on to students in writing classes much of what I had learned from Sam—including those wonderful names— "Dittenfass" and "Trallefass"—that he always used for characters the rest of us might have called "whosis" or "so and so." . . .

And now it seems appropriate to close with Sam's favorite toast: "God help us all."

RALPH STEINER

Steiner was a noted photographer and filmmaker, whom I first met in 1935 at the Greenwich Village apartment of Paul Strand, another famous photographer, as they planned the shooting of Pie in the Sky. *Steiner had graduated from Dartmouth in 1921 and spent his last years in nearby Thetford, Vermont. Remarks at a memorial service for Steiner at Marlboro College in Brattleboro, Vermont, November 15, 1986:*

Ralph returned to filmmaking in the mid-sixties . . . without major sponsors or collaborators. He now lived in Thetford (Vermont) and our lives touched again when he came often to the Dartmouth campus to show his films and to use his experience, his philosophy, and his wit to shake up the students in my classes. He was, in fact, very critical of the academic approach to teaching in this creative medium, his thesis being that successful stimulus to creativity must come from within and not from without.

He was embarked on a series called *The Joy of Seeing* and he showed his new short films as he finished them. *Look Park* was one of them and it was shot in Northampton (focusing on a small waterfall) where the father of his wife, Caroline, had been president of Smith College.

I don't know how many films Ralph actually completed in this series, but his objective was to use his camera to remind us that we are surrounded by ordinary things very much worth looking at if we just make the effort to look closely. One of his movies concentrated on the classic shapes of laundry swaying in the breeze behind an inn on Monhegan Island, Maine, where he and Caroline had a summer home. Another, *Glory Glory,* repeated shots of an irrigation sprinkler shooting sprays of water against a blue sky to six different musical backgrounds, demonstrating that music affects our feeling and what we see is, in turn, affected by what we feel.

The last, called *Slowdown*, is the only one to use camera tricks—undercranking to make a car seem to go 3,000 miles an hour on a country road to contrast with a beautiful landscape viewed at leisure. This is Steiner at his most didactic, saying "What's the hurry?"

I do know that the difficulties of distribution ultimately forced him to abandon the project and to put aside his movie camera and editing table. But, as with his marvelous photographs, which are on exhibit in galleries all over the country, the films made in the thirties (including *The Plow That Broke The Plains* and *The City*) will keep his unique spirit and talent alive.

APPENDIX B

Author's Credits

FEATURES

1932   *Divorce in the Family* (MGM)—joint story.
1936   *We Went to College* (MGM)—joint screenplay.
1937   *They Gave Him a Gun* (MGM)—joint screenplay.
       Bad Man of Brimstone (MGM)—joint story.
1938   *Sharpshooters* (Fox)—joint story.
1939   *Jennie* (Fox)—joint screenplay.
       Winter Carnival (UA)—joint story and screenplay.
1940   *North of Shanghai* (Columbia)—joint original screenplay.
1941   *Dancing on a Dime* (Paramount)—joint screenplay.
1942   *Call of the Canyon* (Republic)—joint story.
1947   *Song of the South* (Disney)—joint screenplay.
1948   *So Dear to My Heart* (Disney)—joint adaptation.
1949   *Cinderella* (Disney)—contributor to story.
1950   *Gallant Bess* (Crestview)—story but uncredited.
1952   *The Detective* (British)—Alec Guinness as Chesterton's
       Father Brown—uncredited joint screenplay with Thelma
       Moss, who shared credit with the director, Robert Hamer.

SHORT FILMS

1934   *Dartmouth Days* (MGM)—director (theatrical short).
1945   *Brotherhood of Man* (UPA)—joint story for animation,
       with the subject sponsored by UAW/CIO.
1951   *My First Week at Dartmouth*—writer and director (re-
       cruiting film for that college starring Buck Henry, then
       an undergraduate).

1952   *Spare the Child* (UPA)—cowriter (under a pseudonym)
        with Sam Moore (animated theatrical release).

1952–   *Magazines in Drugstores* (Transfilm, N.Y.C.)—A pro-
1975   motional animation film for *Life*—with Moore.

        Changing American Market (Transfilm)—A promotional an
        imation film for *Time*—with Moore.

        Calling All Salesmen (Transfilm)—A promotional animation
        for *Life*—with Moore.

        Big Change in World Markets (Transfilm)—based on a *For-
        tune* article and sponsored by First National City
        Bank—with Moore.

        Hello Hanover (Pelican, NY)—promotional animation film
        for McKesson-Robbins—with Moore—directed by?
        J.Zander.

        The Computer Comes to Marketing (Wilding, NY)—This
        was based on a *Fortune* article and sponsored by an ac-
        counting firm, Ernst and Ernst—I wrote and directed,
        with actors in 35 mm.

        The Salesman Isn't Dead; He's Different (Dynamic Films,
        NY)—based on a *Fortune* article and sponsored by IBM.
        I directed it from a screenplay written with Sam Moore.

        The Era of Radical Change (Dynamic)—based on a *Fortune*
        article and sponsored by Armco Steel. I wrote and directed
        it.

        150 Years of Growth (Transfilm)—I wrote, produced, and di-
        rected for First National City Bank. Arthur Ornitz (ASC)
        was the cameraman.

        Energetically Yours (Transfilm)—animated film shown on na
        tional TV for Esso's fiftieth anniversary. Written with Sam
        Moore, with design by British artist Ronald Searle.

        Don't Paint It like Disneyland (Dynamic)—produced for
        Ford Motor Company as an indoctrination to their as
        sembly line.

        How Do We Get There from Here? (Dynamic)—I wrote and
        produced this for the American Trucking Association; it
        was sponsored by Eaton Company of Cleveland.

        Not Relief But Release (Dynamic)—I wrote and directed this
        for the International Institute of Rural Reconstruction.

        Slavery and Slave Resistance (Dynamic)—I directed this for
        the *NY Times' Arno Press* educational film series on black
        history. It featured Cleavon Little.

Auto Mechanic and Technician (Dynamic)—I wrote and di
rected this as a recruiting film for Ford Motor Company.
It was remade five years later to follow up on those re
cruited.

Man of Action (Transfilm)—animated film about urban
blight for the American Committee to Improve Our
Neighborhoods and paid for by Continental Can. Writ
ten with Moore.

Run Fast, Run All Day (Dynamic)—about the 1971 Indi
anapolis 500, sponsored by Ashland Oil. I wrote it and su
pervised the editing.

The March of Time (Transfilm)—comic slide film about the
Time sales force—written with Moore.

Information Explosion (Dynamic)—promotional film for
Cowles Communications. I wrote it and supervised the
editing.

And many more whose titles I forget for such sponsors as:

American Cancer Society
Saturday Evening Post
Family Circle
Life, Fortune, Time, and *Architectural Forum*
American Iron and Steel Institute
American Society of Friends
Jewel Tea Company and Liberty Mutual Insurance

There was no personal credit on the above films during the fifties. My
first screen credit was on *The Computer Comes to Marketing* in 1960.
Thereafter, my name appeared.

TELEVISION CREDITS

1980   *Gnomes* (produced and directed by Jack Zander). This is my
only listed TV credit. It was written with Sam Moore and
was shown twice in a one-hour time slot on CBS.

Others, also written with Moore, but using pseudonyms:

Two episodes of *The Adventures of Robin Hood* (1955–
1958) with Richard Greene ("The Bandit of Brit-
tany" and "Flight from France").

One episode of *The Adventures of Sir Lancelot* (1956–1957) with Robert Shaw ("The Ruby of Radnor").

Two episodes of *Colonel Humphrey Flack* (1958) featuring Alan Mowbray.

We also worked on *The Buccaneers* but I don't think our stories were produced.

PUBLICATIONS

I started as regular contributor to the review section of *Life* magazine in 1967 or thereabouts and continued—with Richard Schickel—as a regular movie critic until the magazine folded in 1971. In 1968, I began a monthly column of movie comment for *Family Circle* and continued for about three years.

My articles and book reviews have appeared in *The Nation, Action* (magazine of the Directors Guild), *Dartmouth Alumni Magazine, The Screen Writer*, and *Quarterly Review of Film Studies.*

Index

About the Author

Maurice Rapf grew up in Hollywood where his father was one of the founders of MGM. He went east and was graduated from Dartmouth College in 1935. He returned to his alma mater in 1966, founded Dartmouth's film studies program, and is now Director Emeritus of Film Studies and an Adjunct Professor who teaches *Writing for the Screen* every winter term.

Rapf worked as a screenwriter in Hollywood from 1936 to 1947, was twice secretary of the Screen Writers Guild, and set up the Guild's arbitration system for credits, which is still in effect. He has credit on thirteen movies; his last produced assignments for Walt Disney include *Song of the South, So Dear to My Heart,* and *Cinderella.* A victim of the Hollywood blacklist, Rapf left Hollywood in 1947 and never worked there again.

He wrote and/or directed forty or more sponsored films for major U.S. companies, was a film critic for national magazines, and has three children: Joanna Rapf, a professor at the University of Oklahoma; Geraldine Rosen, an editor at St. Martin's Press; and William Rapf, head of the art department at Souhegan High School in Amherst, New Hampshire. The author has made his home in Hanover, New Hampshire, location of Dartmouth College, since 1971.

Back Lot was written from memory aboard a Blue Star freighter between Los Angeles, Australia, New Zealand, the Fiji Islands, and Seattle, Washington.